Do your parents:

- criticize all the time?
- open your mail?
- nag?
- drink and get mean?
- refuse to let go of you?
- favor your sister or brother?

These and many other topics are discussed in Help: My parents are driving me crazy!, an informative book that will help you understand many of the conflicts that take place daily in your home.

HELP!

My parents are driving me crazy.

Jane Marks

ace books
A Division of Charter Communications Inc.
A GROSSET & DUNLAP COMPANY
51 Madison Avenue
New York, New York 10010

Help: My parents are driving me crazy!
Copyright © 1982 by Jane Marks

ISBN: 0-441-32744-3

An Ace Original
First Ace Printing: May 1982

Published simultaneously in Canada
2468097531
Manufactured in the United States of America

For Bob, Josh, and Chris . . . with love.

TABLE OF CONTENTS

ACKNOWLEDGMENTS

The following chapters appeared, in different form, as magazine articles:

Chapter 10.   "Breaking the Bickering Habit," *Seventeen Magazine,* November 1977.

Chapter 20.   "Laughing, Crying and Throwing Things," courtesy *Glamour*. Copyright © 1972, by Condé Nast Publications, Inc.

Chapter 22.   "Divorce in the Family," courtesy *Glamour*. Copyright © 1975, by Conde Nast Publications, Inc.

Chapter 23.   "Adjusting to a Stepparent," *Seventeen Magazine,* June 1976.

Chapter 24.   "When One of Your Parents Is Dying: Helping the Family Get Through It," courtesy *Glamour*. Copyright © 1973, by Condé Nast Publications, Inc.

Chapter 31.   Quotes by permission. "Family and Couple Interactional Patterns in Cases of Father/Daughter Incest," by Maddi-Jane Sobel (Stern), A.C.S.W., and Linda C. Meyer, M.A. Chapter XV of *Sexual Abuse of Children: Selected Readings* (published by Office of Human Development Services).

PREFACE

Does this book have answers for you?

That all depends. If you have only *perfect* parents, then the answer is no. But if, on the other hand, you're like the rest of us, then you know how aggravating it can be to deal with a parent who:

- criticizes all the time.
- tries to control your choice of friends.
- tries to keep you a child.
- pries and spies and opens your mail.
- seems to prefer your brother or sister.
- never has time to talk to you—or listen.
- expects too much of you.
- keeps the phone under lock and key.
- hovers.
- won't forgive you for a past mistake.
- acts weird in front of people.
- drinks and gets mean.
- drinks and gets sloppy and embarrassing.
- tries to make *you* be the parent.
- is dying.
- nags.
- doesn't know how to be an adult.
- tries to make you feel guilty.
- took off.

- married a turkey.
- won't give you room to make your own mistakes.
- refuses to let go of you.
- is in jail.
- makes you feel silly or inadequate.
- can't hold a job.
- committed suicide.
- does too much touching and kissing.
- acts two-faced.
- tries to be a pal instead of a parent.
- gets angry—and loses control.
- leans on you too much. . . .

Then the answer is most emphatically YES.

We have some answers, insights, ideas, suggestions, strategies, and sources of outside help.

Whether the tensions in your house are the kind that erupt with all the heat and violence of a Mount St. Helens, or whether they're the kind that merely smolder, making everybody feel depressed and empty, there are ways you can learn to head off the worst of the havoc—and cope very nicely with the rest.

Chances are, you already have the empathy and the good common sense you need to grow up (and even stay sane) *in spite* of all the confusion, perplexity, frustration, and heartache you might have to overcome in the meantime.

YOU HAVE THE BASICS. This book, in the chapters that follow, will help you to fill in the gaps and develop a coping strategy that works.

INTRODUCTION

Even in the happiest of families, there is bound to be some conflict, disappointment, anger, and grief as you begin to substitute your own ideas and values for the ones your parents have always fed you. And it can be overwhelming.

Some days it might seem as though your parents are the most inflexible, intolerant people in the world, determined to keep you on a leash forever. Or maybe it's the frustration of having them insist on treating you like the person they *imagine* (or hope . . . or fear) you are, instead of the real you.

Maybe one or both of your parents are suffering from problems that threaten your freedom and peace of mind; sometimes a parent is ill—and so handicapped or preoccupied with the illness that *you're* left feeling miles away and all alone.

The first section deals with the kinds of power-struggles that teenagers and parents get into, with several hints for understanding and dealing with the real, lurking tensions underneath; how to bring them closer to appreciating *your* point of view, instead of just opposing you on principle.

The second section covers the personality quirks that parents have—the ways they manipulate and control that quite understandably drive you wild and make communication with them very hard, if not unthinkable. Plus, some very useful ways of cutting through all the disagreeable stuff to learn how you can see them—and accept them—in more human terms.

The third section describes the different kinds of tragic, heartbreaking situations that problem parents can put you in—problems that more young people than you might suspect are facing every day. We've gathered some excellent phone numbers and addresses, as well as other usable suggestions for getting you on top of the problem, instead of vice versa. We also try to get to the heart of the matter, in helping you think about what sort of resolution you can hope to achieve, or, in other words, exactly *where* all this is getting you.

PART I: THE POWER STRUGGLE

(Or, getting them to see things *your* way for a change.)

Maybe it worked pretty well when you were younger —just going along and accepting their rules and their point of view on most things. But now, the trouble is that the unquestioning-acceptance routine doesn't make sense anymore. You are evolving rapidly into an adult, an individual related to—but quite a bit more than—the sum of who your parents are and what they've taught you.

This separateness of yours is a fact of life that even the most enlightened parents have some trouble accepting; and so when you begin to assert your independence (and your wish for more) the results can be stormy, to say the least. Some days it might seem as though you and your parents can't agree on much of anything.

Perhaps, just because *they* are the ones with all that official authority, *you've* been feeling like the automatic underdog in most of the skirmishes. Maybe you feel like you have to give in all the time; or maybe you try to act tougher and louder and meaner to let-them-know-you-mean-business—and hope they don't punish you for it.

Something has to give. But don't make the mistake of assuming that it always has to be you!

In the eight chapters that follow in this section, we've sketched out some of the classic bones of contention to show you that once you look objectively at each of the mini-issues (or nonissues) that your parents hassle you about, you can develop a basic approach that is **nonbelligerent, nondefensive,** and yet, **certain to help you win a lot more ground than you ever thought you could.**

Chapter 1: THE MONEY CRUNCH

("They're keeping me at the poverty level.")

Money. It's been called a lot of things; everything, in fact, from "the root of all evil" to "bread" (the staff of life). It can be a source of pleasure and security—or the exact opposites. And there are probably no two people in the world who would agree on the best or most worthwhile order of priorities for spending it.

In families, the money and its distribution can cause plenty of misunderstanding and resentment. *Having* money gives us a sense of control; *not* having enough makes us nervous and angry and ashamed of how it makes us look in the eyes of other people. So it's bound to make you feel angry if you're convinced that your parents are holding out on you, making *you* poorer than the family circumstances warrant.

Two cases: Cindy and Will.

Take Cindy, for example. She deeply resents her mother's rule that Cindy must get permission in advance for everything she wants to buy. Even then, her mother scrutinizes everything ("even underwear") and usually grumbles that something or other is "a waste of money." Cindy dreams of getting contact lenses to replace

1

her glasses (with the same frames she's had since she was ten).

On top of it all, Cindy is convinced that she does "a lot more than my share" of the housework, which ought to be good for something in terms of buying power. What rankles most is that she feels her parents are purposely using their power of the purse not to keep expenses down in general, but to keep Cindy "in her place"—i.e., completely dependent.

Then there's Will, just beginning his senior year. His parents had always been extremely generous, but out of the blue his father told him, "No, you can't get a class ring. Sorry." No explanation. At the same time, his mother stopped bringing home his favorite treats from the supermarket. "You don't need to fill up on that junk food," she muttered. "Eat a vegetable for a change, and skip all those nitrates anyway."

Will is, understandably, confused. He figures he must have done something (or failed to do something that he should have done), as if holding back the money is his parents' way of letting him know they're displeased with him. "What else *could* it be?" he wonders. His father has this terrific job, drives a Cadillac . . . .

Underneath it all, there is an explanation, and contrary to what Will thinks, the austerity campaign is not to punish him or keep him on his toes. In fact, it has nothing to do with him.

It has to do with his father, who is suffering from deep embarrassment. "How do you tell a kid that the big bad wolf is at the door and about to come in because you've failed as a provider?" his father wonders. He lost his "terrific job" to a young assistant two months ago and all at once found himself without *any* prospects, and unable to cover the basic expenses. ("And when you can't simply open the checkbook and pay the bills, you feel

cut down to size—like how can my son respect me anymore?")

So both of Will's parents have been keeping up a front for Will's sake, trying not to let their son suspect how things really are. Of course, Will's mother seems on the bring of tears a lot these days; and Will's father loses his temper a lot.

It's too bad Will's parents can't trust more in Will's ability to understand that what has happened to his father was not the result of stupidity or inertia, but a crunch of circumstances, a setback, one of those things in life that can't be predicted or controlled.

Even now, after many painful days of silent misunderstanding, it still isn't too late for his father or mother to say to him, "Look, Will, here's what happened, and we've got to deal with it like three adults. I know you like roast beef, but tonight it's rice and beans, which are

nutritionally adequate—and not bad the way they're
jazzed up. Is it humiliating? Come on, Will. Think of all
the rich people who go out to Cuban restaurants and
think it's a treat to have what we're having. Things will
get better. But for now, we've got to face up to this *together.*" Will might still be disappointed, but at least he
wouldn't be feeling the added pain of bad-little-boy-
being-punished.

What about Cindy? Well, in her case it happens that
she could be right about her parents' sub-rosa "reasons"
for keeping so tight a grip on her spending. Maybe
they're afraid of "spoiling" her, or can't face the idea of
letting her make even a simple clothing purchase on her
own. Perhaps one or both of them experienced such deprivation (real, or even imagined) when they were
young, and are inadvertently doing the same to Cindy.

What she could do is sit down with her parents and
attempt as calm and rational a talk as one can manage
about family and personal finances. If she described her
overall spending needs and gave them a chance to let her
know exactly what the constraints were (in terms of both
budgetary limits and their own gut feelings of what's
proper and adequate for a young woman in high
school), she would be ahead of the game. Even if she
couldn't have all she wanted, she would *know* the
absolute limits (vs. the bendable ones) and, most important of all, she would not need to experience each "I-
want-to-buy-something"/"No-you-can't" confrontation
so intensely as **a personal rejection.**

Do either of those stories sound a little bit familiar to
you? Have you tended to invest a lot of resentment in
the money-flow when it *doesn't* seem to flow in your
direction: TAKE HEART.

You can dream of the day you'll finally be a full-fledged grown-up out on your own, earning your money and having *complete* say over what to do with it. But even RIGHT NOW—regardless of whether your poverty situation is more like Will's or like Cindy's, regardless of why the purse strings are drawn more tightly than you think they ought to be—**you don't have to sit around feeling deprived and powerless.**

If the fast-food eateries, local shops, and businesses aren't hiring, there's always baby-sitting, caring for neighbors' pets and plants when they're at work or away, or tutoring in anything you're good at—from backgammon to baking, music to gymnastics. Run errands, wax cars, rake leaves. Sew hems, type, bartend at parties, organize children's outings or a play-group for Saturday mornings. Paint fences, houses, posters, blighted trees, or t-shirts to sell. Use your time, energy, talent, and imagination, and you *will* find that you have much more earning power than you ever suspected.

Chapter 2: WITH STRINGS ATTACHED

("They give me everything—except my independence.")

Psychologists say that the real formula for happiness isn't a matter of a warm puppy, nor is it having a bottomless expense account with the folks. Rather, the experts say, a young person who has faced problems and managed to work through difficult stress situations (including insolvency) may end up feeling a lot better about himself than a "lucky" kid who's had only good things happen without any particular effort on his or her part.

It may seem strange when you're feeling particularly poor in the cash-flow department, but there are teenagers who suffer from *over-generosity* on parents' part:

- *"My father is always handing me $20 bills for no reason. I tell him, 'Thanks, but I don't need this'; he doesn't listen. I never spend it, just keep it in a drawer of my desk."*

- *"I really envy my friends who get excited saving up for something they're dying to have. I just feel guilty knowing that I could have anything I want. All I have to do is show my credit card."*

Why should this be a problem?
The problem is that even if parents don't realize it,

there *are* strings attached. The lavish support puts unspoken obligation on the young person to behave in a certain way: to be nice, to be pliable, **to be dependent.**

Not that it's done maliciously, or even with conscious awareness. Your parents feel generous and warm. Aren't they giving you everything you could want—*and more?* Never mind that you're left with a sense of uneasy guilt ("Why should *I* have all this? It doesn't seem fair. Lots of kids survive without fourteen cashmere sweaters. I haven't done anything to earn it."). And there's also a nagging certainty that whatever you try to do for your parents, it can never be quite enough. You also wonder: is it to be viewed as bad manners, disloyalty, or outright treason if I go ahead and do something they don't want me to do?

Here are the options you have:

    (1) *Angry confrontation:* "You know what you can do with this check. . ." (Makes everybody feel rotten.)

    (2) *Capitulation:* "Gosh, thanks, Mom and Dad. I realize it was foolish and immature of me to feel that I was really supporting myself this summer. Yes, I know you bought all my clothes, and also that trip before school started." (Makes you feel helpless and angry: doesn't communicate the real you.)

    (3) *Subtle rebellion:* "I'll let them buy me all these clothes, but I'll fix them by living in this one pair of tattered painter's overalls." (Makes parents think you're crazy; doesn't help them understand your point of view.)

    (4) *Honesty and calm:* "Mom and Dad, you are the most generous parents. You give me so much and I appreciate it; but sometimes, I think

I'd be more comfortable having a little less.

"I mean, if you're going to give me **X** dollars a week, couldn't I at least do **X** amount of work around the house? Thanks for being so understanding." (Makes parents feel good enough to be receptive to *your* feelings; also gives you a sense of having gotten things off your chest.)

REMEMBER: It might seem as though they're trying to cripple your budding initiative, but chances are those over-giving parents are trying to live down (or live over) some early money traumas of their own.

In any case, a good way to shore up your drooping self-confidence or get over feeling "pampered," "soft," or "spoiled" is—once again—to go ahead and earn some money of your own.

Chapter 3: TELEPHONE TENSIONS

(A classic hang-up.)

The telephone may be the ultimate way of reaching out across miles and even oceans, but sometimes its very existence seems to *clog* communications with the folks at home. Basically, it's because parents and teenagers tend to look at the phone in such different ways:

THEY see it as a way of getting, or giving, a quick piece of information.

YOU see it as a way of visiting, passing time, re-establishing contact with friends (even if you did see them in school today).

THEY think you should:
- **not** be on the phone all the time (to the exclusion of homework and other useful activities).
- **not** run up the bill with overlong or unnecessary calls.
- **not** demand that everyone leave the room the phone is in to ensure your privacy.

YOU think they should be more understanding, more aware of your need to be in contact, to be—quite literally and most of the time—connected with your friends.

11

What you need is a compromise plan that you and they can live with. For example, you might:

- agree to limit the duration of most calls sharply if they will allow you an occasional long one without carping.
- propose a fair limit to the number of calls you can make per evening—if they will agree not to hound you or give you dirty looks when you *do* go to dial.
- ask your parents to help you identify the specific issues *as they see them*. (Is it the cost? The fact that you monopolize the line so that they can't get their calls? The fact that your phone-life is keeping you from interacting much with the family?)
- agree that you'll keep incoming calls from blossoming into talkathons—even if it means you have to tell the caller that "I have to keep this one short."
- agree to be more reasonable in your demand for privacy when you're on the phone. (Reserve that request for *special* calls, not just the routine gossip/catch-up, which can be done better in person anyway.)
- ask your parents if they would consider purchasing some extra service. The phone company will not install a pay phone in a private home, but an extension phone for your room (which would solve the privacy problem) would cost under four dollars a month. Perhaps they'd consider either splitting the cost with you, or giving it to you as a birthday present. A second line would be more expensive (somewhere between eight and fifteen dollars, if you stick to the basic allotment of message units), but you might be able to talk them into it if you agree to pay for it out of summer earnings, or work off all charges above the monthly maintenance.

Chapter 4: IT'S ABOUT THOSE FAVORED SIBLINGS . . . .

There's no question that brothers and sisters complicate whatever's going on between you and your parents. Whether you're the baby, the firstborn, or squeezed in the middle, it's the presence of the others that somehow intensifies the problem of getting to be who you are.

"Why can't you be more like your brother/sister?"

When the wonder-child ahead of you has already established himself as the official genius of the family, or the "gorgeous one," or the all-around charmer, it can't help but make you feel second-rate, or at best a copycat.

When the older sibling's marvelous qualities are talked about endlessly, it takes a lot of restraint on your part not to make a lot of sarcastic remarks to the tune of, "Sorry, I'm just a mere mortal." The other temptation is to be perverse and try to carve your own reputation in an opposite (negative) way, as "the lazy one" or "the slob" or even "our little no-brainer."

Neither approach will advance your cause. The only really worthwhile option is to say to your parents, "Look, I'm proud of so-and-so *too,* but I am not competing. I am *me* and I'm trying to be the best me I can, and that's the best I can promise."

"I'm me—or can't you tell?"

Some teenagers suffer from the opposite problem—
it's the don't-confuse-me-with-my-rotten-sister syndrome, and it's inconvenient, to say the least.

Take Gina, for example, a very straight fifteen-year-
old who's never given her parents a moment's worry.
And yet, in spite of her thoroughly untarnished record,
she is given a third degree every time she steps out of the
house.

"Look," she says with a sigh. "I *told* you we were
going to a movie over in Rosemont . . . . Yes, it *did* let
out at 11:25. But you know it takes twenty minutes to
drive home from there. Yes, and I'm sure you wouldn't
have wanted Steve to go through any stoplights or
speed. . ."

"We just don't want you to take any foolish
chances. . .," Gina's mother explains for the hundredth
time. Of course—and Gina knows it—her mother is
thinking of the older daughter, Susan, who was pregnant at fifteen, and popping a whole rainbow of pills.
Nevertheless, Gina runs to her room and slams the door
so hard that her framed award for good citizenship
bounces off the wall.

Her parents look at each other and shrug. "That girl
and her temper!" They are truly upset and concerned.
Didn't Susan's bad behavior start with temper tantrums
too, just like this?

As unfair and frustrating as it is for Gina, *she's* the
one who has to do the hard work—explaining, as often
as necessary (but with patience), that sisters do not have
to follow in one another's footsteps; that Susan's problems are Susan's, not hers; that self-destructive behavior
is not in the genes.

"The forgotten man."

Then there's Richard, who is the straight man in his family. It's his brother, Paul, who goes around stealing, skipping school, vandalizing neighbors' property, cutting bushes, spray-painting driveways—you name it. Unlike Gina, Richard has no problem convincing his parents that he's different.

"But so what?" Richard gives an exasperated sigh. "My parents know they can depend on me. But they take all the good stuff I do for granted: my marks, everything, as if I'm expected to do well, period."

The problem? "All they ever want to talk to me about is Paul! I know they work hard," Richard says. "There's not that much time for us to get together and talk. But still, *I'm sick of always hearing them talk about Paul.*"

Richard knows in his heart that it would just be self-destructive and foolish to try to call attention to himself by acting like Paul. Still, he sometimes wonders if that might not be the only way he'd ever get anything approaching equal time.

- *Perhaps* for Richard, the best approach would be to tell his parents how he feels. Maybe they've considered him so much of an adult that they've failed to consider his perfectly legitimate need for some recognition, an occasional pat on the back.
- *Perhaps* they've come to rely on his "sympathetic listening" without considering his needs. Call it a parental blind spot. It might be worthwhile for Richard to tell his parents how he feels; to say, "I'm sure you don't do it on purpose, but it really bothers me that we spend so much of the time talking about Paul. I have ideas and concerns also. Couldn't we *sometimes* take a little time and talk about *me?*"

It might not be the easiest speech to make; but it can accomplish a lot. The fact is, parents—especially tired, preoccupied ones—are notoriously bad at reading minds. In fact, **nine times out of ten they can't know how you feel unless you tell them.**

"Not so helpless."
Problem: "My parents must love my little sister more than me. They never do a thing when I complain about the way she intrudes on my life and my friends all the time, and pesters me to death. They won't even let me lock her out of my room."

Options:

(1) Complaining some more—and driving your parents to side, most probably, with her.

(2) Taking matters into your own hands—creatively. That means approaching your little sister, not to talk tough, but to see rather if you can possibly initiate a friendlier, more mutually pleasing relationship.

You might not feel like it, but if you spend some time with her, you may find her less clingy and desperate to be in on everything you do. Notice her, *cultivate* her. Let her feel that you're interested in her and willing to give her some feedback on her life, some details of your own.

She *is* a fact of your life, and so she might as well be a pleasant one instead of a drag. Instead of using her as something to rail at your parents about, you might even try to make her an ally. Why not? You'll not only feel less smothered, but also your parents will certainly notice the change. Then, how can they help but think, "Wow, isn't he (or she) the diplomat and the resourceful one!"

Another thought:

Do you see yourself getting nothing but crumbs while a more favored brother or sister gets the lion's share of parental attention, privileges, what-have-you? Before you succumb to a terminal case of woe-is-me, or write your parents off as patently biased against you, it wouldn't hurt to look at some of the common reasons why parents might *appear* to be caring more for the other kid, when in fact they aren't.

Gender.   It may seem unreasonable, even silly, in this day and age, but it happens: *"When my brother does something, my parents say, 'That's a boy for you,' but when I do something, they say, 'Girls mustn't do things like that.' I get punished and my brother just smirks."* That girl is angry and jealous—and has every right to be —but does the difference in treatment come from her parents loving her less? No, it's just their outmoded way of thinking, which—once she can see it for what it is, instead of what it isn't—that girl is certainly free to try and influence.

Birth order.   This is another can of worms, offering all sorts of opportunities for feeling left out and underprivileged. Older siblings notice that the younger ones are getting away with murder and assume it's because the parents like them better. Those elder brothers and sisters don't realize that most parents mellow and relax as they get older and more experienced, and *that* is usually the reason why they do let the later arrivals do more things at an earlier age. At the same time, middle children often feel robbed of any clear-cut claim to fame in the family, obscurely wedged in there between the ("over-indulged") youngest and the eldest ("the one with all that status and freedom"). And finally, it's the youngest child in the family who often feels like a non-person, as the one whom the parents will "never take

WHEN DID I EVER SAY THAT PLAYING TENNIS WAS DUMB?

seriously." At least when we know what we're dealing with, we can recognize that grass-is-greener syndrome in ourselves. Then we aren't forced to react to those perceived slights as if they were intended to hurt us and make us feel unwanted.

Interests. Maybe you've started noticing that your father always asks your sister if she wants to play tennis, never you. Is she the number one favorite? Not necessarily. It may be nothing more significant than the fact that you told your father once that tennis was dumb, or that it was too fashionable for your taste, or whatever. Maybe you were even kidding, but your sister's the one he sees outside with her racket, whacking a dead old ball at the side of the house.

Have you ever tried saying, "Hey, Dad, I think I'd like to learn if you have the time to teach me." (It might just put things in a whole new light.)

Aggressiveness: If it appears that your parents spend a lot more time chatting and just *being* with your brother, say, than with you, it might not be so much that they prefer his company; rather, it may be their way of giving you the "space" they think you want. Does your brother get more attention from them because he actively seeks it out, while you tend to be more passive, more private or preoccupied? Do you have a tendency to drag your feet when a family outing or project of some sort is suggested? And when was the last time *you* made a move to *initiate* one?

Chapter 5: "THEY WANT TO TELL ME WHO I CAN DATE."

(Is sneaking the answer?)

So your parents don't think that anyone is good enough for you. It's a common complaint: *"They treat strangers more politely than they treat my boyfriend, Steve—like my Dad had the nerve to put Steve's cigarette out instead of asking him to do it. They don't want Steve to be important to me, but he is."* It's not that the objections to Steve are concrete ones. They might not even *say* what they don't like about him.

So what is it? Some secret fairy-tale image of the sort of marvelous person that you "should" be going around with? An overreaction to the leaping divorce rate among young marrieds? Snobbishness? Fear that you are being wooed away from the traditional values they've taught you? Or is it plain old jealousy: an unwillingness on your parents' part to see you getting deeply involved with someone besides them?

Parents have so many different, altruistic, selfish, valid, and absurd "reasons" for resisting your romantic choice at this point, it seems that each case calls for special handling.

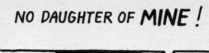

Lena.

Take Lena, for example. She complains that her parents won't let her go out with Gary for the pettiest of reasons—i.e., he dresses like the punk-rock fan that he is, and usually has a safety pin or two in his earlobe. Lena insists that Gary only does it "for fun."

Lena's parents say that she's making a fool of herself and embarrassing them—not to mention the fact that someone as antisocial and bizarre as Gary would probably have no inhibitions about knifing her some day. They say he has to be sick to go around the way he does. She says they have no right to judge him when they've never even met him, but only seen him at a distance. They say "no dates with Gary." Lena screams, "Unfair!"

Actually, Gary hasn't asked Lena out. He hangs around her at school—constantly—and likes to nuzzle with her on the stairwell.

To get through this deadlock, Lena first needs to make sure in her own mind that she's not confusing the issue of wanting to see Gary with the natural adolescent yearning to prove to her parents that she can do what she wants—regardless of whether it bothers them. (After all, going around with a boy who looks "sick" to her parents might strike a lot of people as an eloquent way of saying "phooey" or worse to their conventional or super-straight point of view.)

If, on the other hand, Lena feels sure that Gary's style and appearance are incidental and *not* key to her fascination with him, then she might approach her parents in a pleasant way and ask them if they'd be willing to meet him once, and get a chance to observe for themselves that he is much more than the sum of his safety pins and punk look would suggest.

Since Gary hasn't tried to see her outside of school, there would be little for Lena to gain from any big confrontation with her parents over him at this point. If she can manage to seem more casual and less intense and defiant about liking Gary and wanting to be with him, maybe her parents wouldn't have to resort to speeches and rules about his "type."

Andrew.

Then there's Andrew. His parents suddenly announced one evening that they didn't want him dating any girl who wasn't Jewish. That struck Andrew as very unfair and strange, since his high school and neighborhood were about 90 percent non-Jewish. "Our family has never been religious," he told his best friend the next day. "I don't get it. What's the big deal? I have always had non-Jewish friends and my parents have never objected."

Since the new rule seems to have come out of the blue, it would seem that a frank discussion of family beliefs is overdue. Why, for example, are they living where they are, surrounded by non-Jews, if they don't want Andrew to mix? Has something happened recently to change their feelings? Are they fully aware of the low, low ratio of Jews in Andrew's school?

After listening to what his parents have to say, Andrew needs to explain that they are pushing the panic button needlessly, as he is only fifteen, plans to go away to college in three years, *and* then to law school, and isn't likely, he feels, to end up sticking with and marrying any girl he'd happen to be dating now, anyway.

If they're adamant, he might suggest that the family join (or at least allow him to join) a Jewish cultural organization or a temple, even if it would require a little traveling. That would show them that he's not out to defy them, but that he isn't in favor of sitting around without any hope of a social life, either.

Is sneaking the answer?

Sometimes sneaking is tempting when you're fully convinced that your parents would never accept the person you want to date.

When Heather met Kenny and found him "more like me than any boy I've ever known," she was overjoyed. The only problem was that Kenny was white, and Heather knew only too well that her parents' "superpride" in being black precluded any chance of their welcoming Kenny—or even tolerating him.

At first, she would tell her parents she was going to her friend Betsy's house to study whenever she and Kenny had a date. But as she and Kenny grew closer, the deception made her more and more nervous.

Heather felt unbearably torn: Kenny meant so much to her, but seeing him on the sly was a terrible gamble. She knew that if her parents found out that she'd been dating a white boy *and* lying to them, they'd be much, much angrier—and much more resistant to *ever* accepting Heather's right to make her own dating decisions.

Heather knew that her feelings for Kenny were genuine. (If she'd only been using Kenny to shock her parents, then she'd have been *flaunting* rather than trying to *hide* his existence in her life.) She decided that the best chance of success lay in leveling with her folks—but strategically. She went to her father's sister, someone the whole family felt close to and trusted, and asked her aunt to help her break the ice, to let her parents know that she had acquired a "friend" who happened to be white. She assured her aunt that the family should not interpret Heather's attachment to Kenny as any implied rejection of her heritage; on the contrary, her parents should feel proud to have raised their daughter to be proud of herself, and open-minded enough to recognize qualities in people that go deeper than the color of their skin.

Would they balk? Would they fuss and say, "No daughter of mine . . ." Perhaps they would, at first. But even if they'd never come to love the idea of Heather and Kenny, they *would* be more than likely to recognize that creating a scene would only drive the two of them closer—and drive Heather *away* from them. Perhaps, in the end, they'd even come to grudgingly admit that Kenny really wasn't such a bad guy after all. In any case, Heather would be free to make up her own mind about him without the humiliation, the fear, and the resentment of having to sneak.

Disadvantages of sneak-dating:
(1) Nervous stomach.
(2) Constant fear of getting caught.
(3) Constant need to check up on or bribe any accomplices (such as the friend your parents think you're studying with).
(4) Guilt.

(5) Pressure/strain on the relationship as you start to wonder if he/she is really worth all the plotting, all the anxiety.

(6) Pressure/strain on the relationship as you try to persuade yourself that this person you're out with *is* worth the rift that's developing between you and your folks.

(7) Possibility of losing parents' trust if they find out, or even if they only happen to notice how furtive you've become.

(8) Disappointment in yourself that you didn't have the nerve to speak out honestly and tell your parents in a forthright way that you think they've been too hasty in judging your friend, that you'd like them to give him/her another chance.

Chapter 6: "DON'T I DESERVE A LITTLE PRIVACY?"

("They think they have a license to hover.")

When otherwise rational, well-meaning parents overdo protection beyond anything reasonable, it may not be that they really mean to keep you hermetically sealed off from real life. Some parents seem to snoop and demand to know all because they:

- *think it's their duty* to personally chaperone and protect you from everything that's lurking out there, waiting for a chance to corrupt or take advantage of you—or they . . .
- *are deeply involved* in your life because it's like a soap opera, but more so—or they . . .
- *got in the habit* a long time ago and never thought of doing things differently.

And, sometimes, parents claim that they're justified in hovering; that they have a special reason. **But no matter what their reason, it's up to you to decide if that reason is enough to justify your putting up with it.**

Take Lucy, for example. Ten years ago, when she was six, she was badly hurt in an automobile accident and lost the use of one hand. Lucy doesn't consider herself handicapped; she manages to do everything with one hand. But her mother insists on doing everything for her.

"It can get annoying," Lucy admits sadly. "Mom is always barging into my room to see if she can do anything for me, even when I have a friend over." Lucy adds that she recently found her mother opening a letter to Lucy from a boy she'd met on vacation.

LUCY: "Why, Mom?"

MOTHER: "Oh, my darling. I was only saving you the trouble of tearing the envelope. Did you think I was *prying?*"

Lucy has tried to tell her mother that she's just a bit overprotective; but her mother says, "Nonsense, dear. What else in my life could be more important than taking care of you?" Lucy doesn't push too hard. She understands how terribly, albeit unreasonably, guilty her mother feels for that accident ten years ago.

But does that mean that Lucy has no choice but to go on letting her mother be her right hand?

NO INDEED!

Lucy has already figured out that her mother's hovering over-concern has more to do with mother's needs than with any rational assessment of Lucy's. But there may be more: perhaps Lucy's mother is unwittingly equating dependency (Lucy's) with love; she may feel that she needs to be totally indispensible to Lucy in order to have *any* importance in her almost-adult daughter's life.

It would appear that she doesn't realize (and needs to learn) that giving Lucy *more* independence and *more* opportunity to take care of herself and gain confidence in her ability to do so would *not* harm the mother-daughter relationship, but improve it.

Lucy's current strategy of appeasement—being tactful

and compliant, no matter how outrageously her mother intrudes and takes over—might seem like the safest course. (After all, it avoids conflict.) But the price of allowing those apron strings to remain uncut is much too high.

Lucy claims that her mother is hard to talk to. So she must show her mother that she is not only able to do her own coping, but determined! "I know that will make me feel better," Lucy says. "But won't my mother be demolished?" Not necessarily. If Lucy is successful, her mother will eventually see that Lucy's growing up is *not* such a threat, and that she (the mother) *can* afford to loosen her grip on her daughter's life—without losing touch.

Chapter 7: I MADE A MISTAKE AND NOW THEY WON'T LET ME FORGET IT.

("How can I get them to trust me again?")

LET'S SAY: You broke one of the cardinal house rules, or maybe you did something wildly dangerous, or thoughtless, or stupid.

THEY SAY: "Sorry isn't enough."

YOU SAY: "If only I could turn back the clock and undo this thing."

It may seem like the good things in life are over, the way your parents are saying that they'll never be able to trust you again.

We are certain that you haven't blown it for good.

The question is, how to deal with the consequences now, in a helpful and healing way that makes sense in terms of:

* what's already done.
* the future.
* right now.

The answer may be in developing a good strategy for getting back in your parents' good graces *(without re-sorting to groveling or lying).* Here are some sugges-tions:

   (1) Give them time to cool off, to be mad or sad, *be-fore* you go to work on them.

(2) In the meantime, try to be pleasant and polite, but *not a doormat.* (No matter what you've done, you are entitled to your dignity.)

(3) Try not to *constantly* refer to the thing they're mad at you about. Let it fall into some perspective. In other words, don't let this issue totally dominate and color your day-to-day relationship with your parents. (Remember, you knew them for a long time *before* this happened.)

(4) Don't take the things they say in anger as irrevocable. You know by now that when parents are upset, they may say a lot of things they won't mean an hour later. Chances are your father, for instance, doesn't really intend to "lock you up and throw away the key." But at the moment he said it, he just couldn't think of a more constructive way to show his concern and disapproval.

(5) Put all your tears and histrionics on hold. You can fall apart privately, but throwing a tantrum in front of your folks can only aggravate the way *they* feel. A calm and mature demeanor on your part might, on the other hand, convince them that you:
  ● aren't so immature after all, and . . .
  ● do deserve another chance.

(6) Let them know you're sorry for the pain, inconvenience, worry, embarrassment, expense, or whatever distress your escapade caused them. Give them the feeling that you've learned something. (For parents, *that* can cover a multitude of sins.) Try to explain to them WHY you won't let the same thing happen again.

(7) Don't back them into a corner by reminding them of a threat they made to you in the anger or the anguish of the moment. Give them a chance to

back down gracefully without feeling like they're sacrificing parental honor.

(8) For the future, give some real thought to what happened and why. This is not just for the sake of avoiding their fire and brimstone next time, but also, more importantly, for upgrading your own good judgment.

(9) Be a good sport about accepting whatever restrictions, grounding, or punishment they hand you. There's a good chance that *they'll* relent some if *you* don't push.

(10) Don't make excuses. At this point, they don't want to hear them.

(11) Don't mope.

(12) Ask yourself if the thing you did was a way of trying to get a subliminal message across to your parents—as in:

● "I refuse to conform to your standards . . ."

or—

● "Please notice me and love me on *my* terms. . ." or—

● "Look, I'm afraid I can't measure up to your standards, so why should I try?"

If so, it would be better next time to *verbalize*. Acting it out can seem easier, but in the end, it's your grades, your reputation, your relationship with your parents, and your freedom that you are sabotaging. In other words, you don't have to cut off the nose (yours) to spite the face (theirs) if you can talk about it.

Remember: *Nobody's* perfect.

We all miscalculate at times and make mistakes and need to be forgiven. So you messed up. Welcome to the club! Try not to let this experience turn you into a timid soul. Just because you've laid an egg doesn't mean you're a turkey.

Chapter 8: WHAT IT ALL MEANS— THAT BASIC TENSION THAT WON'T GO AWAY

(Or, what it is you're *really* arguing about.)

You may not be an official adult yet in some people's eyes; but you are way beyond childhood now, and you are naturally impatient to begin taking charge of your own life for a change.

Your parents, on the other hand, are not about to hand you your freedom on a silver plate. It's not that they think you're totally incapable of making decisions for yourself. No, chances are they're very proud of you, and relieved that you've made it this far.

Still, they are concerned, and they may also feel a kind of motherly/fatherly imperative to save you from yourself. After all, they have lived through a few things themselves, and it is hard for people who've nursed you through teething pains and first-day-of-school anxieties to see you as you really are now—grown up, or very close to it.

And, on top of that, they have a big problem: that if they acknowledge that you're as old and seasoned as you are by now, they also have to face the fact that they're much older, too, which is something in this youth-worshipping society we live in that a lot of parents will fight like tigers.

So it may appear to them that they have everything to lose, and the prospect of letting you go becomes *a very sore and volatile issue in itself*. **And that is what is always lurking under those "little discussions" about neatness, for example, or who you're dating, or what you may do when, and who decides.**

In other words, it's this basic tension over who is to be in charge of protecting you and keeping you safely in bounds that is the stuff of which so many day-to-day hassles and arguments are made. If you feel that your parents are consciously or unconsciously afraid that as their watchdog role in your life diminishes, you aren't going to be needing or wanting any part of them, the following strategies may be very useful in getting them to lengthen the leash, so to speak:

(1) *A little forbearance*. Be prepared that you may have to accept some unnecessary concern and control on their part. They *are* still in charge for a while longer, and once in a while, they might have a point. Anyway, the more gracious you can be, the more good-will points you can win (to be used when something really matters).

(2) *A little reassurance*. Make a point of asking parents for advice now and then. Whether or not it turns out to be useful, it will serve to show them that you do value their opinions and that your wish for more independence doesn't mean a complete breakaway/rejection.

(3) *A little parental consciousness-raising*. Demonstrate your evolving good judgment and maturity by (a) doing homework and chores without being prodded; (b) doing unexpected helpful things like taking out trash, folding laundry, washing the dog, unloading the dishwasher; (c) taking on responsibility away from home

through baby-sitting, a part-time job, volunteer work in the community, or some position of leadership at school or in an after-school club or activity.

There is a lot you can do to help your parents update their thinking. They may not be so much afraid of seeing you grow up. They may just be waiting for a sign of it.

GOOD MOVES AND BAD MOVES: A two-part tactical guide for shifting the balance of power your way.

Chapter 9: THE IMAGE.

(Or, how to clean up your act.)

Advertising geniuses found out years ago that whatever they were selling, the way they packaged and presented it would have a major influence on whether or not people would *believe in it and buy it*.

It's the same with parents when you're trying to sell them on your point of view. Here are some Do's and Don't's for "repackaging" *your* product—i.e., *your* demands, *your* complaints, *your* struggle for independence.

(1) **DO** clarify. If you want your message to get across in persuasive and palatable form, take some care to let them know that· your criticism isn't to be confused with (a) REJECTION (as in, "If you're so critical, you must want no part of me," resulting in whipped-puppy sulking *and* nonlistening), or (b) DISRESPECT (as in, "If you criticize me, you are insolent," resulting in indignation, crackdown, *and* nonlistening), or (c) IGNORANCE (as in, "If you criticize me, you don't know what you're talking about," resulting in contempt *and* nonlistening), or (d) ARROGANCE (as in, "If you criticize me, you're spoiled rotten; we've been too lenient as parents," resulting in anger, over-strictness, *and* nonlistening). That is why it makes good sense to think through and know clearly what

you're explaining or complaining about.

(2) **DO** try to be more "all there." When your mother calls you, for example, don't ignore her or say "just a minute," and *then* ignore her.

(3) **DON'T** be afraid it will label you as wimp or turncoat if you trade in a sullen or long-suffering parent-side manner for a whole new stance in which you're noticeably cheerful, polite, neatly dressed, smiling, responsive, and interested enough to ask a question. Pleasantries like "Hello" when you or a parent come home would not be amiss and can stir up a lot of parental good will.

(4) **DO** avoid the appearance of sneakiness, because they'll imagine that you're hiding more than you actually are, if you:

(a) always cover what you're reading or writing when your parents approach;

(b) stop talking on the phone and start whispering or answering in grunts or "ummm's" instead of words when parents approach.

(5) **DO** pay attention to your body language. If you slouch, stare into space, throw a leg over the arm of your chair, cross your arms, or look at them sideways, they will sense indifference, boredom, unreceptiveness, and skepticism, as in, "That's a crock if I ever heard one." Rather, it will *win* you points if you can sit up straight, look them in the eye, and at least appear to be giving them your full attention. (Note: Too much of a good thing, like eye contact, say, is just as off-putting as too little, if it results in a wildly intense and disconcerting stare!)

(6) **DO** follow through. If you ask a question, you must wait for the answer without examining your

cuticles or checking your watch.
(7) **DON'T** snicker or roll your eyes heavenward or otherwise show contempt or make them feel silly. Whatever fleeting satisfaction it might give you, it's the worst possible strategy because it *will* get their hackles up and be used against *you* at some future time.

Chapter 10: TAKING OFF THE COMBAT BOOTS

(Or, how to kick the bickering habit and cultivate the useful art of compromise.)

It's a fact: Sometimes you can win more by avoiding a battle in the first place. Here is some practical advice for breaking the bickering habit.

Sure, it's great to speak up when something *really* counts. But splitting hairs or squabbling interminably about inconsequential points is strictly another matter. Bickering isn't self-assertiveness. It doesn't clear the air; it doesn't win you points for goodwill or respect; and even when you're itching to have that last devastating word, the actual pleasure of doing so is small and fleeting, compared to the resentment it invariably incurs.

Sure, we all indulge in bickering from time to time. Chalk some of it up to feeling exhausted, fed up, or annoyed with ourselves. "Even beyond the obviously vulnerable moments, each of us has a special bickering pattern," says Dr. Selma Miller, past president of the New York Association for Marriage and Family Therapy. "This means that everyone has sore points or special areas of susceptibility, and if those areas are encroached upon, [he or she is] likely to respond by bickering." One person may do it when he feels unfairly dealt with (and afraid to speak up); another may use it as a defense when she's the guilty one—to forestall being accused of acting inconsiderately. Still another might feel lonely or alienated, and yet act cantankerous toward anyone who tries to come too close. "It's a common problem," Dr. Miller continues. "To want closeness and yet be unable to accept it. Bickering can be a way to keep a 'safe' distance, but if you're that safe, chances are you're inaccessible . . . and consequently isolated."

A good start is just not to give in the next time you feel the old impulse coming on. Perhaps it would help to imagine a monstrous, flashing neon sign that says, "Don't quibble." Of course, we all know that it isn't always that easy, because the temptation to split hairs can often be so compelling that you'll want something more than a mental reminder.

Understanding where that overwhelming urge is coming from can be a much more reliable safeguard. It might be helpful to see which (if any) of the following apply to you:

(1) **Do I bicker because it feels safer than showing that I'm disappointed or angry?** Any close relationship involves some misunderstanding, some bad, embarrassing feelings. Working through them is the way we get to know ourselves—and our parents—more deeply. *Those hurt angry feelings don't just go away,* unless we deal with them by admitting they exist and talking them out. What frequently happens, in fact, is that they come out in other, more destructive ways—and one of them is sullen crustiness. The I'm-hurt-but-I-don't-have-the-right-to-speak-up message picks up many barbs along the way, and it's more likely to elicit a counterattack of a long-suffering sigh than warmth, understanding, or apologies.

(2) **Do I bicker to keep the parents at bay?** "Sometimes," Dr. Miller says, "in a close but weed-choked relationship, we may use bickering to say,

'quit running my life' or 'I love you, but I'm scared you won't take me seriously.' Unfortunately, the messages often come across sounding all thorny, distorting any legitimate concern or criticism into an attack." Stopping and saying, "Hey, what's going on?" is often all we need to make us realize it's fear and not anger that's pushing us to fight.

(3) **Do I constantly rise to my parents' bait?** If so, it can be disarming—and loving—to stop and ask him/her what is going on. That doesn't mean coming on like a shrink with an in-depth analysis, but just acknowledging the problem: "There might be some deeper issue making us (not you, us) a little irritable." The touchiness may be just as much yours as your parent's and it might well be a relief to both of you to be able to speak frankly about it.

Of course, some people seem to invite negative reactions, not because of an intense, stormy relationship with us, but because they feel, unconsciously, that any attention (even getting us involved in pointless combat) is better than the feared alternative of no response at all.

(4) **Do I bicker to get even?** It's always a good idea, when haggling over even the most impersonal matter, to make reasonably sure that we're going after the *issue* and *not the person*. For instance, your mother mentions a film she loved, and you say that you didn't care for it. She says, "Well, you probably didn't understand it." You escalate the struggle by telling her that even her favorite reviewer called it mediocre. Then she says she's enough of an individual not to be swayed by reviews, so *you* say, "You're probably not swayed

by reviews because you don't know how to read!"
Clearly, you've gone way beyond any discussion
of the movie.

(5) **Do I seek my parents' opinions as an excuse to de-
fend an insecure position of my own?** I-talk-you-
listen is the name of the advice-seeking game. Example: You ask your parents if they think you
ought to break off with your boyfriend, now that
you know how irresponsible he can be.

Maybe they try to stay neutral, helping you
to sort out the issues, but hedging about stating
an actual opinion. You beg them to speak up:
"*Please* tell me what to do." They relent and
say, "Well, okay. If I were you, I'd think about
giving him up." You become offended and tell
them that they obviously don't understand
your problem and wouldn't know true love if
they fell over it. Crazy? No. Just another example of the Catch-22 nature of adolescence, of
wanting some guidance or input from them, yet
finding when you get it that it smells too much
like interference.

(6) **What would happen if I didn't bicker?** Ask yourself, next time you're about to pick up the old familiar cudgel, "Do I really need the crutch, the
ego salve, of putting them down?" It just may be
that absolutely nothing would be lost if you sat
back and let the chance for that last word pass by.
In fact, knowing and proving that you can be generous and tolerant, that you can *choose* not to be
picky and petty, will give you a good reason to
feel legitimately great about yourself.

When you know you have a tendency to fly off the handle. . . .

- Your willingness to acknowledge your own part in creating the friction instead of putting it all on your parents is a constructive beginning.
- It helps to analyze what starts it: try to notice what you're feeling (*and* how you're expressing it) next time you see red. Make a list, when you get a chance, of the most frequent sources of conflict: Is it curfew? Neatness? Respect? Money? Ask yourself if there's any way you can offer a compromise without giving up anything that's really important to you.
- You can turn a potential power struggle into a more cooperative search for understanding if you say, "I didn't mean to get so upset. Can we try to talk now?" Then listen—not just to the words, but the feelings they seem to convey. When it's your turn to talk, speak to the issues *that matter to them*. Instead of talking about your frustration, work on reassuring them.

PART II: A FAILURE TO COMMUNICATE

Parents are never as rational as they're "supposed" to be; in fact, they can seem so quirky and difficult that some teenagers simply tune out, convinced that their parents are "too hopeless" or that "they could never understand, so why should I try to talk to them?"

Maybe all you really need is a fresh way of looking at the games parents play, because if you can spot the *real motives or needs* behind your parents' most exasperating attitudes and ways of treating you, then YOU ARE FREE to respond to them in a better (i.e., warmer, less defensive) way—*and with much better results.*

Chapter 11: MARTYRDOM

("They Try To Control Me With Guilt.")

Hank had decided that college wasn't for him—at least not now. "I'd really like to take some time off," he explained to his parents. "This would be a perfect chance for me to get a job, look around, travel. Besides, I'm so bored with school right now—it's just a waste of money if I stay."

Hank's father stares in disbelief. Then he shakes his head uncomprehendingly and turns away. "An opportunity his father never had," he mumbles. Meanwhile, Hank's mother has let out a series of gasps and clutched at her heart.

"Mom!" Hank is alarmed. "Are you okay?"

"Who, me?" she wheezes. "Don't worry about me. I may not live to graduation, anyway. No, Hank. You do whatever . . . whatever makes you *happy*."

Marilyn, at 23, is packing up to move (at last) to a wonderful apartment that a couple of her friends have been sharing since college.

"I'm sorry," her mother says.

"What do you mean, Mom?" Marilyn is taping a carton shut.

"Well, it's obvious. *I* have let you down. I've failed you. I haven't been able to give you what you need."

Mother dabs at her eyes with an already soggy hand-kerchief.

"Oh, Mom!" Marilyn has heard this before. "Don't be silly. You're a terrific mother . . ."

"You don't have to say that!" Mother snaps. "No. I always *tried* to do my best for you. God knows. Never gave you even one bite of food out of a can. Everything fresh. And, oh, do you *remember* how I sold Grandma's ring that time to send you to ballet camp?"

"Oh, Mom." Stricken, Marilyn leaves her packing and tries to put an arm around her mother.

These are fairly typical examples of how the Parental Guilt Machine works: you're damned if you do and damned if you don't. If you go ahead and *do* what you think is right, you're haunted by a sense of having let your parents down in some irrevocable way.

If, on the other hand, you *submit* (as in, "Well, I guess I could stay in for another semester, anyway . . ." or, "Well, I guess I could wait until after Christmas to move out . . ."), you are faced with the sinking feeling that *once again you've been had.* (And you have!)

It can be a very locked-in, no-win situation, until you begin to understand the dynamics of the parent-perpetuated guilt you're up against—and what you can do to *weaken,* if not eliminate it from your life.

How it works.

Sometimes it's very much out in the open: "What do you mean, you want to borrow the car? You never *did* care a fig for anybody *else's* needs but yours."

But more often, it's more elusive, tucked-in; *sneakier,* the way parents use the old "feel-like-a-crumb-or-a-criminal" technique to manipulate their grown-up children. "It's all right." (BRAVE SMILE.) "I can take most anything," carries the suggestion that:

- your selfish, irresponsible, thoughtless, devil-may-care, arrogant, me-first, narcissistic, insensitive, outrageous, insufferable, heartless behavior is chronic.
- you are the chief cause of his/her extraordinary suffering.
- you are totally ungrateful for all he/she has done for you, given up on your account, and had to miserably endure on your behalf.
- you are stuck with feeling bad about all that *forever,* since there's no way you can ever *repay* the parent or make it up for having "forced" him/her to stay (miserably) married all these years for your sake; for having "forced" him/her to sacrifice important career (and attendant fame and fortune), luxury, and youth—all to give you the excellent nurturing that you required.

(OF COURSE, IN REAL LIFE, CHILDREN DON'T "FORCE" THEIR PARENTS TO DO ANYTHING. BUT

DON'T EXPECT A PARENT WHO'S WORKING YOU OVER TO ADMIT THAT HIS/HER CHOICES WERE MADE BY HIM/HER, NOT BY YOU.)

What have you done to deserve all this garbage?

- *Maybe* you've been inconsiderate.
- *Maybe* you've done nothing more than daring to disagree, to grow up, to get out from under.

It's a pretty good assumption that the parent who does this sort of thing on a regular basis is *not* doing it for fun or by choice. Rather, we suspect that he or she is *also a victim of guilt:*

- *Struggling* with his or her *own* heavy load of parent-perpetuated guilt.
- *Feeling so diminished* by its long-term effects that the parent can't realize that you would ever take his/her advice or spend any time with him/her if you didn't have to—and so he/she keeps *you* on the hook via guilt, which is stronger than any galvanized, fireproof, super-strong chain you can find in the hardware store. In other words, they pick this way to hang on because they're afraid you'll disappear otherwise.

So, it's a pretty good bet that there's a rather pathetic "Don't grow up and leave me" message amid the harsher implication that you are an overworker-and-underappreciator-of-parents, and that you're trying to skip out too soon, without having *paid in full!*

You didn't invent this problem; and there isn't a whole lot that you can do to erase all that martyrdom and placate the parent. What you can do, though, is work on getting yourself disentangled.

DON'T act defiant. (That only ends up making you feel like a Rotten Person—and reinforcing the whole guilt cycle all over again.)

DON'T try to make everything all right by "giving in

a little," or even a lot, in a futile effort to barter for your freedom. Something as precious as *that* is not something that parents (and especially parents who feel deprived or threatened) are going to hand you.

DO remind yourself as often as you need to that you're *not* a bad person and you're *not* treasonous and you're *not* cruelly and permanently breaking all ties with your parents if you decide to exercise *your* judgment and *your* free will—and wing it without your parent sitting on your head, directing you.

DO help your own cause by avoiding situations that are likely to fill you with additional guilt. That's the last thing you need. If, for example, you've promised to mow the lawn or scrub the bathtub or take your grandfather to the dentist, then *do it*— and do it as promptly as possible. If you promised to do it last week and forgot, then make your apologies and make your amends. A good rule of thumb, if you want to get off the guilt-go-round, is that it takes less effort to do the things you're supposed to do than it takes to keep on feeling remiss.

DO curb the sometimes *very* tempting impulse to repeat the pattern with your friends. In other words, keep yourself vigilant to feeling "wounded-but-I-won't-give-you-the-satisfaction-of-admitting-it." (Remember how much *you've* hated that routine.)

DO stick to your guns! Sometimes giving in may look like the sane, pragmatic thing to do. (Look how it *seems* to reduce all that tension—for now.) But it's just like giving in to a toddler's tantrum, in the sense that you're only telling your parents that the guilt technique works!

Believe it or not, **your parents will survive** if you:

- go out tonight—even if he/she was counting on your company.
- accept that scholarship you've wanted—even if it means going to Timbuktu, and not getting home for both Thanksgiving *and* Christmas.
- cut your hair—even if the parent has "loved it" long.
- grow your hair—even if the parent has "loved it" short.
- join a religion or political party if it makes a great deal of sense to you—even if the parent is convinced that you've just joined up with the devil himself.

They may get mad, turn red, keel over, turn purple, cry, or refuse to talk to you. But in the end, it will be your own quiet determination to liberate yourself that will make it possible for you to have any kind of decent and enjoyable relationship with them.

Chapter 12: FALSE FRONTS

("Why won't they say what they mean?")

Two-faced—or unaware? Whatever you choose to call it, a lot of different parents, for a lot of different reasons, seem to have a devil of a time expressing themselves. It's not that they don't speak up; they do. But *when* they do, the *words* don't match what are on the faces and in the hearts.

It's as if they've put their feelings and opinions through a processor so that these "truths" are distorted or completely obscured by the time they come out. And that can leave you in quite a bind—trying to figure out just where you stand and what the message is that you're supposed to be getting.

It's entirely possible that parents who do it don't realize that they're doing it. For many of them, it's been a life-long habit. (Especially if they had parents who encouraged them to keep the real stuff hidden, as in "Of *course* you don't hate your little brother!" or "You should be *happy*, not sad, that Daddy's safe in Heaven" or "Tell Aunt Sophie how much you adore that pink and turquoise angora outfit she made for you.")

But as far as you're concerned, having to try and decipher hidden meanings lurking *under* the face value of what parents say can end up making you feel:

- **DUPED.** ("Boy, was I a patsy! They said they

WHY CAN'T THEY JUST SAY WHAT THEY MEAN?

didn't *care* what marks I got as long as I tried my best. Well, I really believed them. I *did* my best. In fact, I busted my chops. But I still ended up with B's and C's. They're mad—*and so am I*. From now on, I don't think I'm even going to bother trying to please them.")

- **CRAZY.** ("I must be nuts. I can *see* that my father is mad about something. He keeps saying he isn't. I don't know what's wrong with me.")
- **SHOCKED.** ("My folks always spouted this liberal stuff—what a hero Martin Luther King was and all that. But I thought they'd both have *heart attacks* when a black guy asked me to a college weekend. I mean, all these years I thought that was what they wanted.")
- **FOOLISH.** ("They're always praising my musical talent, so-called, telling me how great I am. But when I volunteered to be part of the entertainment

for a big anniversary party they're having, my Mom turned pale and said, 'Uh . . . uh . . . uh . . . I wouldn't want to *impose* on you.' She looked stricken!")

Why do they do it?

- They might be too ashamed of the truth.
- They might *wishfully think* that they *are* liberal, tolerant, as aware of your feelings as they pretend to be.

But in any case, it creates gigantic communication-blockage when your parents' *talking words* are out of synch with the *inner voice*. Here are some classic examples.

(1) *DO AS I SAY, NOT AS I DO.* Mike's parents have always touted honesty as the best policy. He's believed them, and generally acted accordingly. (Once, when he was five, his father spanked him publicly in front of his friends for having lied about spraying his little sister with the garden hose.) So it bothers Mike tremendously now when he hears his father brag to a friend about how easy it is to get away with calling the family Mercedes "a business expense" on his tax form.

Mike also feels bad when he sees his mother do nothing and say nothing when the cashier at the deli gives her an extra five dollars in change by mistake.

"I guess they think the great honesty-policy that they hammered in me doesn't apply to *them*," Mike fumes. "If they've lied to me all these years about the Great Value of Honesty, I guess they've lied about everything. I'll just have to start taking *whatever* they say with a big grain of salt—or a shakerful."

(2) *I TRUST YOU, I TRUST YOU.* "That's what they *claim*," Mae grumbles. "But then why do they try to sneak a peek at my diary when I'm out walking the dog? And why do they cancel their plans to go out at the

last minute just because I tell them that my boyfriend's dropping by to return my typewriter that he borrowed?''

"It's not that we don't trust her," they'd say if anyone questioned them. It's just that they're desperately afraid that if Mae and her boyfriend had the opportunity, they'd be sleeping together. They don't want their daughter to have to bear the emotional responsibility of a sexual relationship. (They're convinced that she isn't ready.) They are also afraid that she would get pregnant.

Mainly, they are unwilling to relinquish their control over their daughter. They don't think she's mature enough to make an intelligent, correct choice. *The problem is* that they are afraid to level with Mae and tell her of their fears. They don't want to make her mad or alienate her. So they say, "Yes, yes, of course we trust you," while, at the same time, they check up like a pair of nervous jailers.

(3) *I'LL BE THE ONE TO DECIDE WHO YOU ARE.* Tracy's parents are both first-generation European immigrants' children who've made it by any all-American standards of success.

Lately, Tracy has begun to watch her parents very carefully. She is trying to get an accurate "identity-reading" of how well *they* feel they fit into the American dream, how much they still identify with their "old-country" customs and origins. But all Tracy can glean is a kind of stop-and-go confusion that leaves her feeling frustrated—and sometimes humiliated—by her parents' lack of candor over their own ambivalence.

"I can't tell whether they want me to look and talk like the preppy kids at school in their alligator shirts—like, are they *proud* of me for getting invited to play tennis with Muffie Frothingham at her parents' country club—or will they act like I'm being disloyal or pretentious, hanging out with that group?"

On the other hand, when Tracy displays some interest

and curiosity about her roots, or asks to cook an ethnic dish, her parents can't seem to decide whether they're pleased or disgusted. And Tracy feels embarrassed.

If only Tracy's parents could talk about their own mixed feelings and conflicts in reconciling their two "worlds," then Tracy would be free to explore and search for her *own* comfortable place.

(4) *OF COURSE I'M NOT MAD.* Walt *hears* his father say it, but there is that unmistakable frost in the air that tells Walt that everything isn't fine. Walt's father probably has no idea how tough his phony denial is making it for Walt. The father thinks: "Walt would think I was being petty if I admitted to him that I'm sore about the mud he left on my golf shoes, which he didn't even ask if he could borrow."

Maybe Walt's father is afraid of opening up that whole can of worms. Or maybe he needs to believe for his ego's sake that he is "too nice a guy" to get mad. The trouble is, his insincerity and coldness (because of *unexpressed* resentment of Walt's inconsiderateness) end up much more punishing to Walt than a reprimand could ever be. Also, this way, Walt *doesn't know what's wrong* and, uninformed, may do the same thing again. If his father could say what's on his mind, even angrily, at least it would be an honest expression and the air would be clear.

(5) *I NEVER GET MAD.* That's Jackie's mother's motto: she prides herself on having such perfect control that she never even *sulks,* let alone yells. A paragon, right? But maybe she hasn't created such an emotional nirvana at home after all.

Her super-determination to suppress every single hint of hostility she feels (and her great skill in doing so) leaves Jackie (an ordinary mortal) feeling ashamed, inadequate, and sometimes rotten-to-the-core.

Why? Because learning to acknowledge and handle

one's own negative feelings is an important task of becoming an adult. When you have a parent who never, ever displays even a flicker of wrath, you don't get to *give yourself permission* to have (and express) some of those maybe-unattractive-but-universal-and-entirely-human feelings.

(6) *YOU'VE JUST FAILED THE LOVE-TEST*. This one's a specialty of parents who insist on viewing themselves as "flexible," "easy-going," "undemanding."

"I don't criticize and I don't ask anyone for much," Pam's father announces, puffing modestly away on his old briar pipe. But Heaven help Pam whenever she fails to meet her father's *unspoken expectations*. Like Walt's father, Pam's will not get angry; he'll just feel betrayed, unloved, and totally sorry for himself. Pam can't decide whether to be irked at her father for not having *told* her it was important to him to have someone home in case his office called, or guiltily sad with such a modest, unassuming, *undemanding* person. Either way, it's a "game" she can never seem to win.

What should you do when your parent believes that a "party-line" or "false front" is better than genuine feelings?

- You can try to *gently* poke the "real" underlying issues out of hiding but be careful not to push too hard, as that will only send them deeper underground.
- You can trust your own gut feelings and tell it like it is, even if your parents can't seem to.
- You can try to recognize, and fight against, any tendency in *you* to be a cover-upper; remember, the more you do that, the less of a chance you have of people understanding you (i.e., the REAL YOU and not some bland imitation).

Chapter 13: THE WORRYWARTS

(Parents who let their anxieties undermine your self-confidence.)

They probably started doing it when you were a baby, during your earliest exploring. Maybe you wanted to see what a cat or a mud puddle tasted like. But before you'd gotten a chance . . . .

"No!"

"You'll get hurt!"

"You'll get germs!"

"You'll get all messy!"

"NO, NO, NO!"

Well, it wasn't that they meant (or mean) to wreck your initiative and make you too fastidious and fearful to let your curiosity, ambition, or sense of your own unique, unfolding destiny guide you.

Sometimes, when parents pull the nervous-nellie routine, it can sound like they care more about what other people think than they care about you, as in, "Are you sure you can't get a ride home with *someone* other than that greasy-looking fellow with the acne and the junkyard car? What if someone thinks he's your *date?"*

Sometimes worrywartism can look like a cruel put-down of you and your ability, as in "Well, dear, I *know* they said encouraging things in the admissions office when you went for your interview. But maybe your Dad should ask around among his friends to see if anyone

knows one of the trustees of the college who could be
persuaded to write a letter about you."

(Or . . . . "Why bother trying out for———? I mean,
it's out of your league and you can only be hurt.")

(Or *even* . . . . "Honey, are you sure you're even going
to be able to *find* the place? In that neighborhood, with
all those *trees?*" I'd sure feel better if you called it off.
Besides I've heard it's a very *unfriendly* campus. Snobby.
Big brains. Not like you, honey.")

What it seems to add up to is a constant, jittery warn-
ing that:

- YOU ARE IN OVER YOUR HEAD.
- YOU ARE HEADED FOR A FALL AND YOU
  DON'T EVEN KNOW IT. (But I will do my best
  to save you from the disappointment, pain, embarrassment, and comeuppance that is surely in store if
  you follow your own inclinations.)

It's not much fun to live with this kind of attitude on a regular basis. If you're not careful, parents like that can make you just as fearful as they are, just as dourly convinced that:

- YOU ARE UNPREPARED TO FUNCTION WITHOUT BENEFIT OF APRON STRINGS.
- THE WORLD ITSELF IS SO DANGEROUS AND QUIRKY, SO OVERWHELMING, THAT BEHAVING IN AN INDEPENDENT, OPTIMISTIC WAY IS ONLY INVITING DISASTER.

Some super-worrywart parents tell their children, "Don't have dreams because then you're safe from disappointment." That *is* playing it safe—but so is living in a cage.

There is no guarantee in life that:
- last night's date will call this afternoon.
- last night's date will call—ever.
- you'll be chosen for the wrestling team (even though you know you're a better wrestler than Dan or Woody).
- you won't go ice-cold paralyzed at the audition.
- you'll make it through the job interview *without* saying something dumb.
- the class won't sleep through the report you worked so hard on.

But then again—it might work out *exactly* right. And remember, you have the right to stick your neck out, because, after all, it *is* your neck.

It's up to you!

The net result of having nervous-nellies for parents can be terrible or fine or even better than fine, depending on you. That kind of attitude in parents can nip most of your hopes and ambitions in the bud, if you allow it to, or it can provide you with just the adversity you need to galvanize yourself and get going: striving, persevering, and *believing in yourself.*

Sure, it's hard to pursue a goal—or even the task of growing up and out—without parental backing and support. But think of the alternative (i.e., staying put). Don't you think your goals deserve your best efforts *before* you shrug and say, "Well, I didn't really want that anyway"?

Here's a basic plan for coping with worrywart parents:

- **DON'T** waste time and energy trying to persuade your parents that you *can* take the pressure of carrying an extra course, or put up with the super-rigorous cheerleader practice schedule. *Show them.*
- **DON'T** accept their doubts about what you can and can't accomplish as gospel. *(They* don't know how much drive and spirit you've got inside you!)
- **DO** branch out. If your parents can't tolerate uncertainty, find someone who can. Seek the advice, enthusiasm, and objective, knowledgeable feedback you need in a teacher, a coach, or someone else who understands what you're trying to do. (This is not to snub your parents, but to let them—and you— off the hook.)

The point is this: if your parents are chronic discouragers, you must be careful not to let them and their attitudes become an excuse for you to be apathetic and do nothing.

Take that calculated risk (as long as it's a calculated one).

- If things go badly for you, don't fall apart. You had a right to try and you did your best, which is all anyone can ask.
- If things go well for you, don't gloat—just enjoy the satisfaction you've earned.

Either way, it helps if you can keep in mind that they,

in all likelihood, are not putting you down or acting on any objective assessment of your chances for succeeding.

Rather, what you're getting is a basically well-meaning, but nevertheless distorted, opinion based on:

- *their* exaggerated sense of danger.
- *their* exaggerated "need" to protect you from dangers.
- *their* mistaken idea that it's possible, or desirable, to keep you wrapped in cellophane.
- *their* own personal frustrations and history of disappointment, failure, and humiliation.

Chapter 14: THE FAULT-FINDERS

(Perfectionist parents who focus on your weaknesses and never see the good.)

- *"My father is such a perfectionist. He's always sizing me up—and finding me lacking."*
- *"My parents are perpetual grouches. No matter how well I do, it's never enough. If I get six A's and a B, they'd say, 'Why the B?' "*
- *"I come home from college for the weekend, and my mother doesn't say hello; she says, 'Look at your hair. What's happened to your hair?' "*

It's awfully hard to feel good about yourself when the folks who raised you are always finding something wrong:

- *with what you do.* ("I can't believe you paid all that money for a little piece of junk.")
- *with what you say.* ("Now, *stop* talking nonsense, do you hear?")
- *with what you wear.* ("Just because it's the style doesn't mean it looks right on you," or, "Those jeans make you look like a hooker.")
- *with what you eat.* ("That's the most ridiculous diet I've ever heard of," or, "Don't be silly, *nobody* has wonton soup for breakfast.")

They might even try to nail you by association, as in, "Well, your friend may *be* as nice as you say he is. But his mother *has* been married three times."

When parents are constantly acting as if you were just
some poor, pathetic, ignorant, incompetent, second-rate
screw-up, it can make you angry, and, even worse, it can
make you start to believe that you *are* what they say you
are. It can even make you start believing that *they* are
omniscient types who always know and do everything
right.

Are they? (Are you kidding?) Actually, they might be
very impressive people; but we suspect that deep down
inside, they don't feel very good about themselves. If
they did, they wouldn't have to pick on you the way they
do, and they wouldn't have their egos all wrapped up in
pointing out your shortcomings and "perfecting" you.

By focusing on *you* and *your* faults (big, little, *and*
imaginary), they don't have to feel so small, so inadequate, so very imperfect themselves. So the problem is

really more with them than with you. (You're just getting the brunt of it.)

The way they got that way: probably, when they were growing up, there was someone who had some rigid standards and exaggerated expectations that they couldn't meet.

This is the time for you to break the cycle. You might not be able to *change* their style or get them to be more relaxed and accepting of you; but at least you can *reduce the impact* of all that downgrading criticism on YOU.

Survival strategies:

(1) AVOID BEING A DOORMAT. Each time you're criticized, try to evaluate the content of it. Sometimes, it is almost certain to be justified (and possibly even *useful,* even if it's given in a tactless way). But if you honestly feel that it *isn't* justified, try (in a most diplomatic way) to point out or explain the *validity* of what you are up to. For example, *"Dad, I can see that you don't think much of my lawn-mowing job. I understand your concern, but I disagree with you. In my opinion, this is a very good summer job for me. It's outdoor work and it's keeping me in shape. Besides, quite frankly, I'm enjoying it a lot more than sitting around in your office, not contributing much of anything and feeling like a parasite. And, Dad? I realize I've only been at it for two weeks. If, at the end of the summer it turns out I've been wrong, I'll be the first to admit it."*

This is real communicating. It's hard to do, especially when you're more or less used to hanging your head in mute agreement. Making the effort to explain yourself or correct the fallacy will help you to nurture those young, tender, *good* feelings about yourself.

(2) AVOID DEFENSIVE ARGUING OR COUNTER-COMPLAINING. For example, let's say they've just made you feel two inches high for having

forgotten to water the African violets, which are looking dried out and bedraggled. What if you were to come back with, *"Well, so what? You forgot to stop the milk delivery when we went on vacation the summer I was twelve. God, it was sour. Remember how bad it smelled?"* That might make you feel better, for a moment, but it really wouldn't do you any good. It would *not* make them feel benign towards you and it would *not* impress them that you really are mature and trustworthy in spite of this one thing you forgot to do.

In fact, this is the very same holier-than-thou attitude (i.e., putting someone else down in order to feel better about yourself) that *they* do all the time that makes *you* feel resentful. A much better approach would be to say, *"Gee, you're right. I should have watered the plants and I feel bad that I didn't. It was a mistake, but you can be sure I won't let it happen again."*

(3) CHECK YOURSELF FOR ANY POSSIBLE DEVELOPING TENDENCY IN YOU TO BE A PICKY, TACTLESS, SUPER-CRITICAL, KNOW-IT-ALL WITH YOUR FRIENDS. For example, if your friend Leslie has just described the terry-cloth and satin poodle-pillow that she wants to give her fiance's grandparents as a present, you might want to say, "Holy God, it sounds incredibly tacky. Do you want to make a fool of yourself?" But you could say something more along the lines of, "Gee, it sounds pretty. But you know, since you haven't seen their home yet and their . . . uh . . . color scheme, you may want to play it safer and bring them something like cheeses." That way, you are not so obviously setting yourself up as the super-arbiter, and you're *not* trampling on someone else's self-esteem.

(4) CHECK YOURSELF FOR ANY POSSIBLE DEVELOPING TENDENCY IN YOU TO BE A PICKY, TACTLESS, SUPER-CRITICAL, KNOW-

IT-ALL *WITH YOURSELF*. Try to let your spontaneity grow without "editing" everything you say or analyzing everything you do to the point where you can't have
any fun and can't be satisfied with anything you do.

(5) DEVELOP YOUR OWN FIRST-AID CARE
FOR THAT PARENTALLY-WOUNDED EGO. For
example, when your parents' own problems have caused
them to diminish your good feelings about yourself, it
doesn't do you any good to just sit there, licking your
wounds—or even to get mad and stay mad. What you
really need to do is *arm yourself* with all kinds of ego
propper-uppers. We mean things like:

Focusing on the things you know you do well. Even if
it's something simple, like keeping your notebooks neat,
or putting colors together, or knowing how to make
someone laugh. Tell yourself, out loud, what you've
done that makes you feel good. Keep a list of these, and
add to it whenever you notice something else. You'll
have it for reference when you're down in the dumps.

Accepting your imperfections. A philosophical attitude, and a sense of humor, surely help when you're
painfully aware of some shortcoming and tempted to
throw yourself away, or write off the whole package because of it.

Giving yourself a challenge. You don't have to climb
the World Trade Center, but if you can pick an area in
which you feel slightly unsure of yourself—like talking
to adults, for example—*imagine* yourself being as
vivacious and relaxed and charming as you wish you
were. What would you be saying? How would you act?
Imagine the scene in detail. You can even get in a little
practice. For example, next time you go to the drug
store, don't mumble. Say, "Good morning, how are
you," to the counterperson. Start a mini-conversation.
Smile. Remember, you're a charmer even if you haven't

reached your full potential yet.

Keep it up until it feels so natural, you can talk to adults—*any* adults—with ease and confidence.

Chapter 15: DISTANCE-MAKING PARENTS

("They just aren't there for me.")

It's very frustrating and painful to feel like you're always at the *bottom* of your parent's list of things to do, as if you're supposed to manage—and thrive—on practically no attention.

But before you conclude that the situation is hopeless, you might take the time to distinguish which of the three major *strains* of the STEP-ASIDE-KID-I'M-TOO-BUSY syndrome you're dealing with. For example, the mildest one is the WORKAHOLIC; then comes the CARDBOARD CUTOUT; and finally, sadly, the most intractable of all, the FROZEN-HEARTED.

The point is that each of the three requires a particular approach if you want to get out of the rut. Then, once you know which type, or combination of types, you're dealing with, you know how to proceed.

Type I: The WORKAHOLIC, or "How can I compete with that overstuffed briefcase?"

Despite the various canned soup and frozen casserole commercials on TV that make career-involved parents look not only important, but also ever-so-serene, available, and animated with the family, it isn't necessarily the case.

In real life, it's an altogether different can of soup. Working parents tend to come home late and tired and grouchy more often than not. Some of them actually bring home even *more* work to do after the supper dishes are cleaned up (if not before), or maybe, instead of coming home at all, there's just a note or a phone message telling you to make yourself a sandwich, and don't forget to do your homework, and lock the door before you go to sleep.

Parents, in epidemic numbers, are afflicted with this fever of the times—to work, to bust their chops working, with little time or energy left for anything else. In some families, it is an absolute necessity to work so many hours. Plus, parents who are doctors get emergency calls in the middle of the night, and deli-owners, presidential advisors, locksmiths, police officers, and reporters may have to work evenings more often than not because it's built into the job.

But what about the many, many parents who *choose* to work when other people are presumably home with their families? What's in it for them? It would be too simplistic to say it's money, since many workaholics already have more money than they need. Maybe they feel they need to do even more work and earn even more money in order to feel worthwhile in their own minds— as if they have to compensate for imagined "laziness" or "stupidity" that they're convinced they suffer from.

Maybe those over-working parents are deeply committed to what they are doing. Maybe they need the constant praise or gratitude or fame that comes with the work. Maybe they're afraid of having leisure time and not knowing what to do with it.

Whether or not you know what's causing the one-track bind in your workaholic parent, it is natural for you to feel forlorn, rejected, and angry. You might even be tempted to use that parent's unavailability at home as an excuse to:

- *waste the time* that he/she isn't there to supervise.

- *do poorly* in school ("He/she wouldn't notice anyway . . .").
- *go overboard* on spending ("He/she *says* this working sixteen hours a day is all for the family. Well . . .?").
- *get "even"* by acting indifferent and cold to that parent (actually widening instead of narrowing the gap).
- *become apathetic.*
- *get in trouble.*

Of course, none of those really stop the loneliness or get you what you really want—which is more of the work-addict's time and attention.

Getting to the heart of the matter—ploys that can work:

- *Recognize* that your workaholic parent is unlikely to change his/her stripes, so you might as well try to adjust to the reality instead of dropping a lot of hints about how early your best friend's parents get home from work.
- *Make the most* of the time he/she is not around to be with friends, hobbies, projects, or just contemplating *without being nagged or hassled.* (Think how many of your friends would consider it a gift.)
- *Make the most* of the time that nose-to-the-grindstone parent *is* available to you. (Have the boring chores done and turn off the TV. It will make the time mean more.)
- *Be enterprising.* You don't have to settle for distance when he/she is frequently out evenings or out of town. Slip notes or drawings into his/her attaché case, overnight bag, or whatever. We know one savvy seventeen-year-old who sticks a self-addressed, stamped postcard into her father's shaving kit whenever he has to travel with the tennis team he coaches.
- *Share his/her world.* (It's got to have something

compelling in it!) There are library books available on virtually every line of work, no matter how esoteric or specialized. Read, and ask questions that show real interest. Let the parent know that you appreciate some of the importance of what he/she is doing. You might get invited to spend a day or part of a day with him/her on the job.

- *Be willing* to acknowledge the stress you feel and the pressure that your parent's excessive and probably self-imposed workload is putting on the family and on you. Be willing to *say* when you very much *need* some of his/her time. You have that right, and chances are even a real dyed-in-the-wool don't-bother-me-I'm-working type of parent *will* rise to the occasion if: (1) you let him/her know it's important and (2) you don't cry "wolf" or do it too often.

- *Don't wait* until the last minute, when something important in your life is coming up and you want him/her to be there. It doesn't make sense to simply fail to mention it until he/she is already committed to something else and *can't* come. (Guilt is of limited use.) Instead, write "Drama production" or "Basketball playoffs" or whatever in your parent's appointment book. If necessary, call his/her secretary to make it official. Then your parent will treat it as a commitment rather than a distraction.

Type II: Aloof, uptight—the CARDBOARD CUTOUT PARENT.

"I wish I could be closer to my father, but he never even bothers to ask me what's going on in my life. I have to suppose that he doesn't care."

"All my parents ever say to me is 'Have a nice day' or 'Get your hair out of your eyes.' The other morning, I said, 'Mom, I feel like I'm going crazy.' And she said, 'Look,

you'd better hurry up or you'll miss the school bus. And get your hair out of your eyes.' "

"I had to learn the facts of life from my friends, who had all learned them from their mothers."

You may feel as if they've tuned you out because they're disinterested in you. But . . . .

Maybe they're preoccupied with a personal problem.

Maybe they're trying to be tactful and give you elbow room.

Maybe they're shy.

In any case, a cardboard-cutout-*seeming* parent may or may not respond to your efforts to bring him/her to life, but it's definitely worth a try.

We suggest that you *do* risk making an approach—but gently. That reticent parent may not know you feel hurt or neglected. Most parents would give their eye-teeth to be closer to their teenage children, but *they don't know how*.

That means that you must *tell your parent how you would like it to be.* Be specific, as in, "Gee, Dad. I'd love it if we could work on the car together on Sunday," or "Mom, could we just share a root beer and talk over the day? I'd really love that."

At the same time, be careful to avoid harping on how dismal things have been up to now. That will only make him/her defensive and interfere with the progress you're hoping to make. If you'd rather not be quite so blunt, you might suggest doing something specific together, like going out for dinner or bowling or just a walk.

Instead of feeling miffed that, "Mom pays for my dance lessons but never asks how I'm progressing," *invite* her to come and see for herself. Let her come to a class or recital. She may not have had a clue, up to now, that you wanted her there.

Some parents have a genuine, but limited, capacity for

intimacy. A lack of passionate, animated conversation with you, however, doesn't have to mean a lack of rapport. If heavy conversation scares them off, then try for some quiet, low-key time together. Be willing to start slow. It doesn't have to be spectacular and wordy to be felt.

Finally, you may have to face the fact that many, many parents—and possibly yours—*are and always will be* too inhibited to be able to talk freely with you on the burning issues that you're dying to get into with them. It's sad, but if that is the case, then they aren't too likely to change; and the sooner you can make peace with that (and maybe forgive them and like them anyway), the better you are going to feel.

Type III. The FROZEN-HEARTED PARENT

"I feel so rejected—and it hurts. My dad is hardly ever home, and even when he is, he treats me like I'm nothing, like I have nothing to say that's worth sitting still for. Well, I do have things to say. I have plenty to say and sometime, somebody is going to have to listen."

"Mom considers me a drag. She's practically said that she wishes I weren't around all the time. Sometimes I hate her. Other times, I wish that she'd stay home for the evening and hug me and kiss me and make me my favorite grilled cheese sandwiches. When she puts on her slinky outfits and starts to go out, I get so upset, I feel like screaming."

To be pushed aside without any "respectable" excuse, like having too much work to do, is about as hard to take as anything a parent can dish out. But, what sometimes *looks* and *sounds* and *feels* like outright rejection of *you, personally,* is really a parent's private, unrelated-to-you, pained shorthand for "ARRGGGH. I JUST CAN'T COPE."

Maybe that terrible remoteness comes from a problem that the parent is struggling with: something to do with work or health, money (or no money), or some person you don't even know. **Also, being unresponsive is often a sign of depression.** Maybe your parent is suffering the throes of menopause—or that infamous period of questioning and pain and regret known as "mid-life crisis" that so many men and women seem to have tremendous difficulty overcoming.

There is hardly anything you can do to alleviate *that* kind of situation. What you can do is hope it won't always have to be like this. Remember that circumstances change and pressures let up; and sometimes, quite unexpectedly, people relax and find they can afford a little more warmth than they could before.

Whatever you do, don't give up on searching for the comfort that you need and deserve. The thing is, you may have to look for it elsewhere—in another relative, say, or a friend's family. If you can find a caring adult you can trust who can respond to you in a way that your own parent would like to, no doubt, if things were different, then you're in good shape, no matter how your parent resolves things—or fails to.

In other words, your parent may have a very small capacity for love at this point, but *you* don't have to limit *yours* accordingly.

Chapter 16: PARENTS WHO PIGEONHOLE

("They make assumptions instead of listening.")

It's lonesome and discouraging to feel that your parents don't know the real you, that they haven't been keeping up with your changes, that they've made a lot of assumptions about you—assumptions based not on what you *really* do or think or feel, but on what they:

(1) WISH you were like . . . or what they

(2) FEAR you were like . . . or what the current media stereotype of teenagers tells them to

(3) EXPECT you to be like.

After all, you are, every day, becoming more and more your own kind of person. It isn't easy to become that person. It takes a lot of *work* and *courage* to accept yourself and the fact that you're not a clone of your parents' ideas. It takes a lot more to keep your parents apprised of your progress.

You may complain:

- *"My parents just don't like to admit that I don't see eye-to-eye with them on every single thing. So they pretend."*
- *"If I choose or decide something that doesn't fit my parents' philosophy, they act like I'm headed straight for hell."*
- *"I wish my parents would* ask *me how I feel instead of acting like they know it all. They just stick my*

83

politics, my views of love and sex, everything, in a little pigeonhole, marked 'Youth'."

BY THE WAY . . . . Parents *are* frequently dense, dogmatic, and preoccupied when it comes to "reading" their young person; but you are the one who can make a big difference in helping—or making things worse. For example:

- Do you make the belligerent assumption that they *don't care* about your feelings (and then retreat accordingly); or do you allow at least for the possibility that they (1) don't understand them and (2) would like to?
- How often do you try to "simplify" by not bothering to explain your feelings?
- Do you make the effort to point out a subtle distinction in the way you see something (as opposed to the way they describe it), or do you just "let it

go" because you don't think they'd get it?
- Do you verbalize only your dislikes and complaints? Or do you make the effort to articulate what you care about and love? What really matters to you?

IN THE PROCESS OF SHARING what's inside you, you may find that *you* have been mistaken in your concept of what they expect you to be like. This kind of exchange won't happen in a single conversation or two; but if you are willing to take an active role in helping your parents get to know the one-of-a-kind person you are, *they* will have more opportunity to understand, like, and respect you; and *you* will get to feel more sure of what is clearly and unalterably **you** amid the flurry of changes.

Chapter 17: THE OVERREACTORS

(Parents who jump to solve problems you *aren't* having.)

Linda asks her mother a simple question about child-birth: whether a mother can really be awake to see her baby born. Next thing Linda knows, her mother's hustling her off to the gynecologist for a birth-control pill prescription. "But, Mom," Linda gasps when told where they're going and why. "I'm still a virgin. I'm not interested in sleeping with anyone yet. I'm only fourteen. And about that question—I was only curious."

Aaron asks his father, a doctor, what, if any, actual proven harm there is in trying marijuana. Aaron's parents, in a state of panic, call up other parents "to take some action," they say. "We have to nip this thing in the bud." They organize a series of evening discussions at the community center—and even hire a local psychologist to run the show.

When Aaron learns that it was his question that got the whole thing rolling, he is amazed. "DAD!" he roars. "I wasn't planning to smoke any. I tried it once and I *hated* it. *Years* ago! What I asked you was just one of the questions on my health and hygiene homework. And since you're a doctor, I thought . . ."

Nor can Jessie make a simple remark to her mother

about feeling depressed without evoking a frantic pep talk (when all she really wanted was for her mother to listen a while and maybe give her a little hug).

NOT THAT IT'S SO BAD, THIS ATTITUDE ON A PARENT'S PART OF WANTING TO GET TO THE BOTTOM OF THINGS. It shows that they care, that they're interested, that they don't take your concerns lightly.

STILL—when it seems that they have no flexibility, no humor, no tolerance at all for controversial subjects, it makes it hard for you to be direct with them about anything heavier than, "How was school?" "Fine." If they're going to amaze, embarrass, or exasperate you with some well-intentioned, but wildly inappropriate display of parental overkill, well, who needs it?

It can be even worse when you ask for an *opinion*—on anything from choosing a college to a shade of eye shadow—and they give it *willingly,* but then turn on you when you don't *follow that suggestion to the letter!*

While you *can* avoid the whole problem by sticking to very superficial conversation and avoiding anything with even a spark of interest, we think that you don't have to throw out the baby with the bathwater, so to speak (sacrificing any opportunity for communicating with them and learning from them simply in order to ward off the super-remedy syndrome).

What you have to do is *clarify;* let them know, right at the start, what you are asking for: input; opinion; a sounding board for your thoughts; some simple, objective, factual information—or something entirely different. BUT YOU HAVE TO BE THE ONE TO SPECIFY, TO SAY. Sure, go ahead and ask your question. But just be sure to preface it in such a way that they won't be moved to panic without cause, and maybe do something when nothing is what you'd prefer.

SOMETIMES parents get too involved in your decisions for a different reason: *not* so much confusion as a "need" of theirs to become (overly) vicariously involved in your life—as if it was their chance to relive their own teen years. They might feel very strongly about your majoring in science instead of phys. ed. (or vice versa). BUT IT'S YOUR LIFE, NOT THEIRS.

Dealing with a parent who has a "this-time-I'm-gonna-do-it-right" approach to *your* decisions can be a real challenge to your *own* gumption, backbone, self-assertiveness, whatever.

WE SUGGEST that if you do turn down their ideas (and, yes, you *have* a right to) that you (1) DO IT TACTFULLY (they have feelings, too). "No, thank you" is a lot easier to swallow and no less clear than, "No, damn you." Also, (2) REALIZE that even if they *are* being pushy, they just might have a point. In other words, if you do reject their point of view, be sure it's a conscious choice and not a classic adolescent-to-parent NO-reflex.

Chapter 18: IMMATURE PARENTS

(The "I'm-tired-of-being-the-grown-up" games.)

Some parents, from the look of it, simply don't have it in them to act like grown-ups. Some of it may be a shade of the old 1960's "political" sentiment that there ought to be total equality between the generations, and that parents who presume to exert some authority are cruel, insensitive oppressors.

Other parents do not consciously *decide* to abdicate the classic (and crucial) role of grown-up in the family. They waive the authority or shrug it off because they can't handle it; they feel awkward, frightened, overwhelmed. And believe it or not, the woods are full of them!

Some of them try to relate to their teenagers, instead, as THE BUDDY-BUDDY (forcing an unnatural and imappropriate palsy-walsy cameraderie). Others come on as THE SIBLING RIVAL (trying to fend off a sense of their own *obsolescence* by getting actively and competitively involved in their *adolescent's* social and personal life). Then there's the SWITCHEROO (where they actually try to reverse the roles, so that the young person will take responsibility for guiding and protecting the parent, instead of the other way around).

So when we talk about ineffectual parents, we don't just mean the sad Casper Milquetoast type, or even the

1950's-style bungling TV sitcom Dad, or featherbrained
Mom. They might not look pathetic at all; in fact, the
way you can often spot them is that they're wearing
trendier jeans than their kids are.

The Buddy-Buddy.

Why is it so intrusive, so disappointing, when a parent chooses to be chummy? Basically, it's because that
parent is serving his own needs and neglecting those of
his son or daughter.

Take Roger, for example. His father is so eager to be
liked that he doesn't dare take any potentially un-
popular stand—on anything. As a result, Roger has no
strong father he can look up to, no principles to test and
pit his own developing convictions against.

It's too bad that Roger's father never considered that
(1) Roger can find lots of *pals* among his own contem-
poraries, but what he needs is an authentic parent-per-
son in his life; and (2) that saying no to Roger and having a consistent policy as a parent *might* lead to conflict
and anger, but that in the long run, the hate-me-now-
love-me-later syndrome builds a stronger bond.

Then there's Rhoda. *Her* mother claims that she is
only showing Rhoda *respect* "in my willingness to share
with her . . ." What that mother does is volunteer a running commentary on her own sex life. "We are more like
friends than mother and daughter," she tells people
proudly. As a young person, *she* could never talk to *her*
mother about anything personal, she says, and that was
sad. Well, perhaps. But *now* she has no idea of the cring-
ing embarrassment she causes Rhoda when she starts
describing the sensational orgasm she had the night before.

"Mom, why do you have to tell me that?" Rhoda
mumbles. But her mother is still unaware of how crude
and distasteful those true confessions sound.

The Sibling Rival. *(Muscling in on my act.)*

"My mother has started doing her hair like mine and borrowing my shoes and sweaters and belts," sixteen-year-old Nina complains. "When we go somewhere together, I know she's always hoping that someone will say we look like sisters. It makes me feel disgusted."

"It's unpleasant when I have to bring a girl home here for some reason," Todd, age seventeen, says ruefully. "My father sucks in his stomach and comes on like Mr. Suave. I want to tell him to lay off, to quit making a fool of himself with *my* date, and just act like a father. Sometimes the girl will say, 'Oh, your father's really charming.' I never know how to answer."

Is it simply a form of flattery when a parent wants to try out your clothing, your friends? Is it a form of approval? Is it some sort of effort to shorten the generation gap when they muscle in that way? No matter how benign and sweet the *intention,* the *effect* is usually terrible.

- INSTEAD OF getting really mad, telling the parent to stuff it, and making everyone feel terrible;
- INSTEAD OF accepting the intrusion and trying to convince yourself that you're really lucky to have such "interested" parents;
- YOU CAN TRY to understand what is going on and what you can do to protect your privacy with a minimum of damage to anybody's ego.

(1) REMEMBER that we live in a nation, and a time in history, in which the accent on youth goes *wildly* overboard, leaving those over forty vulnerable to feeling: panicky, lonely, dried-up, deprived, left behind.

Nevertheless, it is *not* your job to help that parent maintain an illusion that he/she is still as young as you are.

(2) IF HE/SHE INSISTS ON BORROWING, you

can say something tactful such as, "I'm very flattered that you like my taste, and I don't mean to be unfriendly in saying this, but I do feel the need for some privacy and that includes not lending my stuff. If you would like, I'll be glad to go shopping with you. There's a great new boutique that you'd love."

(3) CONSIDER THAT THE FLIRTING with your friends may be a sign that your parent is looking for reassurance—not only that he/she is still attractive, but also that he/she is *in your league,* worthy of you, as good as you are. It may not be so much an effort to compete with you as it is an effort to impress you, to get closer.

While you could simply say, "Quit it," "Stay away from my friends," or "Act your age," it might ease the pressure on everyone if you can somehow let your parent know that he/she doesn't need to impress you in order to earn your love. Taking some time to be with that parent and to let him/her know how much you appreciate his/her *genuinely* impressive qualities might gradually lessen the impulse to cross over where he/she really does not belong.

Switcheroo. (To be the one who's worried about instead of the one to do the worrying.)

Some parents seem to try every way they can to switch places with their teenagers. You might wonder why they would want to give up the "perks" of the job, all that power and authority; but it's usually out of a sense of desperation, as in, "I've got to get off the hook."

Take Susannah, for example. Her mother was 100 percent there for her all the years Susannah's father, severely disabled from an accident at work, was alive and dependent to the point of needing constant care.

It was only after he died that Susannah's mother began to act "like an irresponsible kid" (according to

Susannah). "I guess my mother got carried away by suddenly having all this freedom," Susannah says. "But the way she's acting—going out with all these different men, even bar pickups, and, I'm sure, going home to bed with a lot of them."

Susannah felt confused and quite abandoned by the change in her mother: "She claims she hasn't any money when I ask her if I can go get my hair cut, but she always seems to have money to buy a make-up mirror or go out to her favorite nightspot. She used to be sensible and strict, but now she lets me go my own way, do anything I want to, no questions asked. It hurts my feelings, I can't help it. But the worst part is when I look at the clock and it's 3:00 A.M. and she's not in her bed. I try to go back to my own room and go to sleep, but I can't help worrying that she's in some kind of trouble somewhere. Maybe she's been mugged or raped, or the car has crashed."

Whether Susannah's mother is only in a phase that will run its course, or whether she has such a strong need to grab what she thinks she has coming to her now that she no longer has the burden—and the disappointment —of having to care for her husband, she is clearly doing what she "has to do" right now.

As much as Susannah might wish for, and deserve, a more motherly mother than her mother is currently able to provide, she will feel a lot better if she can believe that:

- empathy for her mother does not extend to taking on that sloughed-off mother role herself.
- the lurid mental pictures she gets at 3:00 A.M. of her mother lying in an alley may be, in part, her own self-punishment for *resenting* her mother and the fact that she (the mother) is never around for Susannah anymore. Once Susannah acknowledges

those (quite understandable) feelings in herself, she
may not need to suffer so much painful anxiety.

- Susannah may feel some pressure to act as custo-
dian, reformer, or guardian angel, but *she is the
daughter, not the mother;* and no matter how poor
she thinks her mother's choices are, she can only
live her own life, not her mother's.
- she may feel disappointed, but the best bet (for
now, at least), would be to look for the warmth,
motherly guidance, and companionship elsewhere
—in an aunt, for example, a friend's mother, or a
neighbor.

Chapter 19: GETTING BACK IN TOUCH

Once you see that it's *your parents'* problems that make them seem cold or detached (and *not* a reflection on you, as you'd feared), **the less you have to take it personally.**

It takes a lot of maturity to be able to see that your parents are not really such *cruel* (or, at least not *intentionally* cruel) people when they act that way, as they are vulnerable humans with weak spots and pain. Once you have that more compassionate view of your parents, there is nothing to stop you from trying to thaw things into a relationship that is *much* more comprehending and respectful, on both sides.

Towards that, we offer a dozen suggestions for **brushing off the cobwebs.**

Extend yourself.

(1) FOR STARTERS. It helps to give up the fantasy of making your parents over in a way that will suit you perfectly. You're stuck with the ones you've got and vice versa; so, instead of wasting your time wishing they could be exchanged, why not try actually *cultivating* them, seeking them out. Open yourself up and also try to learn something about them that you didn't know before. The time and effort that you spend on "Operation Rediscovery" might also pay off in the sense of

helping them see and respond to you in a better way.

(2) BE OPEN-MINDED. When you sit down to talk with them, even about something casual, try not to assume that you already know the "type of thing" they're going to say. At least give him/her the courtesy of paying full attention, *just in case* there's a grain of something useful under the trite and predictable stuff.

(3) BE FRANK. Play-acting is offensive, and parents are not as dumb as they may sometimes lead you to believe. You *can* afford to reveal yourself. (How else are they supposed to even try to understand you?) If they get too personal in their probing, you can tell them in a pleasant way that such-and-such is really too private and difficult for you to talk about. That is certainly going to be more acceptable to them than clamming up, turning surly, or making something up.

(4) USE YOUR OWN VOCABULARY. Try to

avoid pat phrases, quotations, and clichés that don't actually describe anything. Your own spontaneous mode of expression will do far better than any "line" for telling them what's on your mind (even if you have to struggle to find the words).

(5) SEEK CLARIFICATION. If you want them to have a clearer (and more sympathetic) view of some controversial idea of yours that they've put down, you need to ask them to be very specific in telling you precisely what part of it worries or upsets them. They might have trouble pinpointing it, or they might find that it isn't really so unacceptable to them after all. They might still object, but at least, if they drew some wrong conclusions or misunderstood what you said before, there is a good chance for all of you to get it straight.

(6) STAY THERE! If your parent is able and willing to open up to you about something, then you are surely

being taken seriously. *Return the compliment* by trying your best to listen—and listen accurately, to the feelings as well as the words. If, for example, your father says, "Hell, no. I'm not scared of that open-heart surgery coming up," but you can see the terror in his eyes, you don't have to contradict him and say, "Yes, you are, Pop. Sure. Take a look at yourself." But you can try, in a tactful way, to *respond* to his need for comfort lurking under his need to have you think he's being perfectly brave.

(7) LEAVE OFF THE SUGAR-COATING. If your parent tells you he/she is worried about something, don't offer too-hasty, fake reassurance. (It doesn't make the problem go away; it only makes the parent feel that you can't stand to listen to it.)

If your father's upset because he thinks he's about to be forced into early retirement, or your mother confesses to you that she's worried sick about a strange little mole on her breast, you may be shocked, you may be scared, you may not know what to say. But try not to succumb to an easy, breezy, "Oh-I'm-sure-everything-will-be-all-right." In your heart, you might mean, "This is perfectly horrible, terrifying news, and I share your anxiety," but it comes across at best as shallowness, at worst as indifference. Maybe there is nothing to say—in which case, a look, a spontaneous squeeze of the hand, can say what you are feeling far more effectively than any "There, there," or "Gee, you've got to try not to worry."

(8) DON'T JUMP TO CONCLUSIONS. If your mother drops a bombshell, like "Your father has asked me for a divorce," or "Grandma's decided to move out and go live with Claude, her disco dance teacher," it's not conducive to good communication for you to *as-*

sume that you *know* how she feels about the above. (She might, for example, be despondent about your father, or she might be terribly relieved, or some of each. Ditto, the news about Grandma.) Instead of shouting, "Oh, how ghastly!" or "Yippee!" a simple "How does that make you feel?" might help her define and express her feelings.

(9) FOLLOW THROUGH. If you ask a question, it's very important to be prepared to wait and listen *to the whole* answer—even if you've got a hockey game to watch on TV or a phone call to make; even if it seems to be taking a lot longer than you bargained for.

The patience to listen is not a skill to be acquired overnight. It takes time to perfect. But it's great if you can get to the point where:

- you don't tune out to daydream.
- you don't shift the spotlight onto yourself (as in, "Oh, *I* had the exact same thing happen to me the other day. You see, I was standing by my locker, and . . ."). To be sure, it is more fun to talk than to listen; and it's also a lot more interesting to focus on *your* concerns than theirs; but still . . . .

(10) RELAX. You may be tempted to fall asleep, slip away, offer advice, try to finish their sentences for them, or quote lines of poetry. But listening—*just listening* to your parents—is an almost unbeatable way of learning *who* your parents really are, anyway.

BY THE WAY: If you've *got* him/her talking to you, that in itself is impressive and you must be doing something right.

(11) KEEP PERSPECTIVE. As you work on getting more understanding of exactly what it is that makes your parents tick, try to remember that none of the effort you're making is wasted even if you find that a lot

of the problems will *not* be solved. Whatever you've ac-complished—no matter how little—is very much to be proud of.

Chapter 20: DON'T SKIP THIS CHAPTER! LAUGHING, CRYING, AND THROWING THINGS

(The problem isn't *having* feelings; it's learning to live with them.)

It may seem, from this section you've just read, that feelings are the stuff that get us in trouble, make us slaves, make us fools, make us miserable to be around. **Actually, the problem isn't *having* feelings.** It's failing to understand and make peace with them. One way you are luckier than your parents is that you are more sophisticated about feelings than their generation was, and you have the advantage of knowing that **just letting yourself acknowledge that you feel something—no matter how freaky or unacceptable it seems—is excellent insurance against its becoming master of you, and making you do things to people that you'll come to regret.** *Laughing, crying, throwing things: how and why to loosen up so you won't have to repeat your parents' quirks.*

Life would be much happier if we always felt what we were supposed to—if only we could produce a thoroughly appropriate emotion for every occasion, and in just the right shade of intensity! There'd be no secret elation at a friend's failure to get into the college that you can't afford; no murderous rage at the woman on the bus who steps on your new suede boots and doesn't apologize. You wouldn't have to fight back a maddening urge to laugh at your relative's funeral, or squelch a whole circus of interesting sexual fantasies.

But since you're human, you're beset like the rest of us with all sorts of emotions that don't conform to a nice civilized pattern. Since feelings are by their nature unbidden and sometimes unpredictable, it's a mistake to hold yourself morally accountable for them—especially when you consider the fact that a strange feeling doesn't necessarily dictate a strange course of action. NOBODY BUT A PSYCHOPATH HAS TO ACT ON AN EMOTION JUST BECAUSE HE/SHE FEELS IT.

Letting it out. Certainly it's harder to know what you're feeling when you're accustomed to keeping all but certain selected emotions under wraps. Anthropologists say that complete emotional spontaneity is not encouraged or tolerated in any society, but the degree to which a person is taught to hold in or deny his feelings varies.

Some anthropologists claim that Haitian peasants are able to express themselves quite freely, while Hopi Indian children must learn to squelch all incipient temper tantrums if they want to meet the agreeable and relatively passive Hopi ideal. In the United States, we have a pretty strong tradition of holding ourselves in.

The shame of it. In many cases we're taught to be ashamed of our feelings. Many people can only let themselves feel things in a depersonalized or disembodied way, as when they're high or tripping and "not all there." Some teenagers tend to respond wildly to favorite film stars and to music, but be very cool and guarded in the "real world" with one another. It feels safer and besides, it's socially sanctioned: look around, at the adults, men and women, who'll sneer at a friend's idealism or softness, and then privately go to a treacle-laden movie and cry like babies.

We are brought up to feel that we ought to be full of good will toward all. We're taught that aggression is bad, rather than to regard it as something necessary to being an effective and distinct human being. And we're apt to suppress and therefore not know that we feel some ambivalence in even our closest and most loving relationships.

Strangely enough, we're also rattled by our onslaughts of good feelings. Haven't you ever felt embarrassed at being confronted by your best impulses—altruism, kindness, honesty, unselfishness—when somebody says, "Huh, a boy scout!" or "What a Pollyanna."

Even with all our informality, as a nation we idealize the containment of feeling. Years ago when President Kennedy was shot, it was traumatic and shocking for the whole country, if not the world; and yet everyone so admired President Kennedy's widow for not crying in public.

Would it have been immoral—or rude—for her to have cried? Obviously not. It's just that the national collective Puritanism in us tends to associate the stoicism of the dry-eyed young widow with courage, and even more, with upper-class breeding and dignity—as though emotions are essentially primitive and childlike, to be found among lower-class and ethnic types, and even a little tacky.

- Good manners and self-control are so "correct" and admired that we sometimes let good breeding cover up for an emotionally constipated need to keep people at arm's length.
- Pride in self-reliance can be used to deny our need for another's love.
- Being polite and considerate can be a rationalization for not standing up for yourself, for being a doormat.

It's only in the last twenty years or so that young middle-class Americans have insisted on granting emotions a reality equivalent to that of more tangible, familiar "goods."

Unfortunately, feelings long neglected are not quick and easy and painless to produce. Their suppression is one of the biggest obstacles to self-knowledge. What is suppression? It's our unconscious, automatic tricky sleight-of-mind for keeping ourselves in the dark about what we are feeling.

Some people—frightened by the nature or depth of particularly confusing and "dangerous" feelings—will try to brush them off like so many incriminating flakes of dandruff. But feelings don't vanish just because you don't want them around. If you refuse to let them into your conscious awareness, they always manage to find someplace to go.

Hiding from feelings is hard and thankless work. You probably know some of those very serene-*looking* people who rarely show a ripple. They don't have much fun because so much of their energy and attention is riveted on the job of concealing what they see as a freakish and terrible nature; and they don't even realize, half the time, that they're doing it.

Actually, all of us—no matter *how* liberated and self-accepting—do some suppressing. There are so many different ways to do it. Glenda's an illustration of one; she suppresses her feelings of jealousy and abandonment and thinks she's really happy when her roommate gets engaged—but she can't figure out why she's overeating again.

Jamie, who's always had his heart set on going to his brilliant father's alma mater, is only willing to admit to himself that he's "a little disappointed" when he gets a flat rejection. (The full extent and intensity of his disappointment, which he *couldn't* afford to acknowledge, is still rankling, *and* giving him stomachaches.)

Then there's Sibyl, who's always so "sweet" that she's

constantly being imposed on by her three college room-mates. Periodically, she feels anger—at the cigarette burn (unreported) on her favorite skirt from the last time someone borrowed it, or the disappearing hair-brush (or vanilla fudge ice cream, or whatever she bought and they helped themselves to . . . again).

But before the anger gets a chance to simmer, Sibyl disavows it. She thinks, *what an immoral person I must be to feel so angry. What if I'd unleashed that anger, it might do something drastic to them. If they ever found out, they'd hate me and they'd get another roommate and leave me all alone. I'd better start being nicer to them.*

At that point, Sibyl no longer feels anger—or much of anything.

There are so many Sibyls around, all convinced that any assertiveness or indignation makes them so danger-ous (and consequently so vulnerable to being deserted by one and all) that they go way overboard in the altruism department—unknowingly, but unmistakably, inviting every bore and parasite in town to take advan-tage of them.

Rather than resolving or getting rid of anything, sup-pression only masks feelings and worsens the conflicts and irritations that we found too hairy to face in the first place.

More often than not, it leaves you with a rat's nest of anxiety grown way out of proportion to the original feel-ing you suppressed in the first place.

Your feelings and your health. Suppressing feelings can wreak havoc on your body—well beyond the common once-in-a-while tension headache or butterflies in the gut. According to psychoanalyst Dr. Lester Schwartz, people who haven't the wherewithal to deal with psychol-ogical conflicts consciously as such, may experience their emotional life in some physical forms. A warded-

off feeling of loss, rage, or other painful emotion can show up in dizzy spells, aches and pains, cramps, vomiting, chronic exhaustion, insomnia, skin diseases, and a raft of other physical problems.

On the other hand, the folksy notion that strong emotions can make you physically sick was convincingly put to rest by an experiment done at Harvard, in which 124 healthy undergraduates were put into a series of stressful situations while doctors measured their gland and heart activity. The result: the fellows who were able to get angry suffered less physiological stress than the "calm" ones whose bodies had to remain in a prolonged state of preparation for emergency flight or fight, keeping up the discharge of adrenalin into the blood.

Conclusion: Anger is often more dangerous if you insist that you . . . ARE . . . NOT . . . ANGRY!#&*@#!!
Even people without noticeable mental anxiety *or*

physical symptoms might find their disowned feelings showing up through a chronic propensity for losing things or breaking things (including one's bones). And we all know that "Freudian slips" of the tongue or the pen can reveal, most unexpectedly, what we didn't know we were really thinking.

Subtle aggression can take the form of nagging, put-downs, and one-upmanship, often disguised by a phony sugar coating that may or may not fool the world. Seclusiveness and severe shyness, seemingly innocuous, can also be expressions of belligerent hostility.

Also, being super-disorderly, dirty, and vulgar around the people and in the places where it's pretty sure to offend may pose as simply doing one's thing, but it's really as aggressive as a well-placed punch in the nose.

It takes a lot of testing, a lot of dipping your toe into the water first, to get to any satisfying level of honesty and revelation. But it's worth every bit of time and effort. THERE IS EVERYTHING TO GAIN BY BEING FULLY YOURSELF WITH NO MASK ON. IT TAKES A LOT OF COURAGE AND PERSISTENCE TO LET THE PEOPLE AROUND YOU KNOW WHAT'S GOING ON INSIDE YOU, WHO AND WHAT YOU ARE, AND HOW YOUR INNER GARDEN GROWS.

Take anger, for instance. To be able to say, "I won't stand for it!" and act on that, can let you know that you have the right to get angry—and still be loved.

Not that you have to turn every annoyance into a major production. Take Mary Ann, for example. She's irritated at her mother for "acting selfish" and "not paying attention" to what she says. She wants to be "honest," but she knows that her mother is under tremendous pressure and extremely tired.

Mary Ann feels guilty about wanting more attention

—and annoyed for not getting it. Still, to *express* feelings doesn't necessarily mean to take immediate action. It does mean to be aware of what she feels, so she can wait a couple of days and see if her mother starts acting more available once her immediate trauma's over and she's had some sleep. (In any case, that would be a better time to talk about it.)

Throwing things: an overrated "impulse." Throwing things in anger, slamming doors—or even people, either physically or verbally—might not always be as inevitable and as necessary as their force might imply.

Throwing something is deliberate (the object doesn't pick up your hand); this so-called uncontrollable anger could be redirected to hurling a sofa pillow at the wall—with no sorry consequences later. Some psychiatrists advocate hurling or pummeling inanimate objects on the grounds that it keeps hostile people from doing those things to people.

But none of those releases are necessarily any more effective or more "natural" than sublimating anger in unhostile activity to work off the adrenalin increase in the body.

Cutting grass, weeding, raking leaves, and even jogging or walking it off provide much opportunity for "controlled aggression." In other words, anger wrongly expressed doesn't cure, but anger suppressed long enough can kill.

Funny-ha-ha—or funny-peculiar? You may not have thought of it as such, but humor is an extraordinarily good expressway for anger and other pent-up feelings.

When people laugh together, they are in accord, sharing not only a delight in human absurdity, but also in most cases a release of tension, since a joke usually tickles some of our taboo unconscious wishes (usually of a hostile or sexual nature) without hurting or even frightening us.

If the humor of the situation eludes you, however, don't be afraid to cry. The feelings and fantasies that come out while you're sobbing can often help you define the source of your unhappiness and an effectual course of action to take. Crying allows others as well as yourself to know that you're sad or hurt.

Even crying all alone has its value. According to psychiatrist Dr. Schwartz, emotions have such strong communicative components that even when we think we're all by ourselves in a vaccuum, in our conscious and unconscious fantasies, we're always with someone. In fact, some of us carry around a whole host of inner people. In crying, you might just discover that your tears were meant for someone you secretly wanted to cry to or about.

Faking it. The only real thing we have to fear from emotion is our own illicit use of it. The cowardly lion roars and rants for the purpose of intimidating those around him when he thinks he isn't lovable enough to get things any other way. He is faking the anger and it rarely works.

The insecure joker is another case of the same point, and just as easily seen through. He tries to dress up a cruel attack in a clown's suit. "You're fat and dumb . . . . Aw, can't you tell when I'm teasing, making a joke?"

The straight-man is supposed to feel like a bad sport or a humorless prig if he or she fails to appreciate the "joke" or tries to retaliate. Tears, too, can be disguised acts of aggression to make another person feel guilty for not submitting to our will. Sometimes tears are turned on in a distorted attempt to get close to somebody; but contrived intimacy is manipulative rather than loving, and rarely works, either.

It's been said that "sorrow may be expressed with such violent cries that it becomes unpleasant because it too closely resembles a raucous, personal advertisement. Some people give the impression of competing with themselves in the degree of sorrow they can show." It may produce immediate results, but it builds up a large reservoir of resentment in the people being manipulated.

The bottom line. Does that sound grim? As though there is never a time when we can be off-guard about our feelings? While we don't even know they're there, they skulk about getting the upper hand, and then jump out unexpectedly to betray us. What victims we are!

IT MIGHT SEEM THAT WAY, BUT IT'S NOT. We must listen to our feelings—even the pettiest, meanest, and most frightening. The solution lies in admission, in facing up to all our so-called bad emotions—aggression, hostility, selfishness. They are ours, natural and human and healthy, but they need attention, understanding, and cultivation.

OUR ACCEPTANCE AND USE OF OUR FEELINGS DEFINES CHARACTER, PERSONALITY, AND SELF. Our abandonment of them lets them run wild and, eventually, they overgrow the self.

Whether you find your nature hateful, funny, disgusting, beautiful, or whatever, coming to accept it is the most human thing you can do. IN FACT, WE'LL ALL BE HUMAN IN THE BEST SENSE WHEN WE STOP TRYING TO CONVERT OUR PSYCHES FROM THE UGLY DUCKLINGS WE THINK THEY ARE TO THE SWANS WE THINK THEY OUGHT TO BE.

PART III: HEAVIER BURDENS

(Parent problems/problem parents.)

Sometimes parents get caught up in problems with sweeping and traumatic consequences for the family: a terminal illness, for example; or a pattern of violence—perhaps sexual violence—directed against the son or daughter; a parent in jail; or one who's taken his/her life; a major drinking problem; a devastating divorce; a new stepparent wreaking havoc with the old routines; a mental illness in a parent that's hard to understand—and even harder to live with.

It is natural to feel most horribly alone and frightened when you are facing any one *(or more than one)* of these so-called "unspeakable" problems. It is very hard to sort out all your feelings, much less know where to turn.

Of course, there are the obvious "instant" escapes like getting high in one way or another, or actually running away from home; but those so-called solutions are self-destructive. They don't do a thing to help you understand the problem, much less solve it; in fact, they just end up making everything worse.

Some young people just do nothing; let apathy win. They figure, "Well, life has dealt me a losing hand," and they don't even try, letting the wound fester instead of doing anything to help it heal. Sure, you've got a harder way to go than most teenagers in forming an identity all your own. But that doesn't mean you can't do it (only that you have more work to do). Once you take the bull by the horns, so to speak, and learn what's involved, what you need to do to take charge of your own situation **in spite of what's going on with your parents,** you'll be in the best possible shape. You'll have a legitimate sense of accomplishment in *knowing* you can cope with anything—and emerge all the more compassionate, and stronger than ever.

Here are some of the very difficult kinds of problems with parents that hundreds of thousands of teenagers are having to confront and live with.

Chapter 21: WHEN THEIR MARRIAGE IS IN PIECES—WHERE DOES THAT LEAVE YOU?

(Or, how not to be a pawn in the parent's chess game.)

"Am I the cause?"

Ryan's parents fight all the time and claim, for the record, that it's all Ryan's fault; that if it wasn't for him and the terrible, upsetting things he does, they'd get along great!

Baloney!!

Sometimes, young people accept the uncomfortable responsibility for their parents' disputes by default, because they haven't stopped to question those false premises that keep them tied up in this depressing role. *NEVERTHELESS, NO MATTER WHAT HE IS ENCOURAGED TO BELIEVE, A TEENAGER CANNOT BE THE* CAUSE *OF HIS PARENTS' FIGHTING.* Maybe his room *is* messy; maybe his strange friends, his problems in staying out of trouble with spray paint and neighbors' driveways, his sloppy appearance or some other aspect, leave a bit to be desired, as far as his parents are concerned.

Maybe his behavior does disappoint his parents and make them critical of the way each other is apparently unable to solve the problems and "straighten Ryan out." But at most, all he's doing is adding fuel to an **existing conflict** between the two of them.

115

In short, Ryan may very well need to shape up—and his parents have a perfect right to tell him to do so, and even to tell him how, if they have definite ideas on that. But they do not have the right to tell him that *their* problems with *each other* are in any sense *his* fault.

"Do I need to keep on being a pawn?"

Roger has trouble with the tension between his parents. "It's so *constant,*" he says. "And so public. When Mom stops talking to Dad, she'll say to me, 'Tell your father he's a damned jerk.' My father, on the other hand, will just say nothing. But then later, he'll take me out for pizza and start to sniffle into the anchovies, telling me how nasty and bitchy my mother is and how he'd leave her *if it wasn't for me.*"

What can Roger do? He *can* just quit listening! He can change the subject; or, if necessary, say, "Look, I just remembered that I'm supposed to be at the library now . . . or weeding Grandmother's garden . . . or flying to the moon"—**whatever!**

He does not owe them a captive audience—or the role of silent participant in the please-be-on-my-side battle of the spouses. Roger is *not* required to take sides, nor is he under any moral obligation to listen to his parents' carping out of any presumed gratitude to them for staying together on his account. That, too, is entirely their affair.

"Am I supposed to be protecting or informing on somebody?"

Wendy's just found out that her mother is having an affair. "Mother is not the least bit subtle about it," Wendy says. "She must realize that I know, and yet she doesn't seem to care. What a dragon-lady. Poor Dad. I'm so mad at her! I don't know whether to tell my father or not. It might embarrass him to find out from me. On the other hand, I hate to see him made a fool of this way."

No matter how outraged Wendy feels, this is an area that clearly doesn't concern her. She may feel protective towards her father, but it is not her place to tell him *anything* about what she suspects.

Whether or not her suspicions are right is irrelevant. Whatever she's seen or surmised, her father has doubtless also seen—or chosen not to. She hasn't heard both sides of this—nor should she.

"But haven't they made it my business?"

Talia's parents have "always hated each other, but quietly." Now, Talia says, they've taken to yelling and screaming—every day and every night. Talia says that she can't even concentrate on her homework, much less relax and think about anything else. *"Why,"* she asks her mother when she gets the chance, "don't you go ahead and tell him to *leave this house*. You'd be much better off without him."

Talia feels that by fighting in front of her, her parents are inviting her not only to get involved, but also to actually solve the ongoing ruckus. Still, for everybody's sake, the best thing Talia can do is to keep a low profile, let *them* be the ones to work things out (or not) their own way.

For one thing, the fact that they seem to be "fighting louder" may be an encouraging sign. It may not mean more trouble, but rather that they're facing their problems together more openly than they had been before, not letting them just build up. Talia doesn't need to take a stand, choose one parent, or offer a "final solution." If *she* has trouble being around the conflict, all she has to do is remove herself—study at a friend's house, or just go into another room and turn on a record, or pick up a good book and close the door.

THE BOTTOM LINE.

In any conflict between your parents:

- YOU HAVE THE RIGHT TO STAY OUT OF IT. You may be pressured or tempted to get involved, but instead, why not try to divert at least a portion of your energy and caring *elsewhere*—say, into a hobby or special interest. (It's *got* to be more fun and more productive than *this*.)
- SAVE YOUR PASSION FOR SOMETHING BETTER. It's exhausting to go on providing the stickum for a parents' marriage that's unglued or getting unglued. Don't try to be a buffer. First, despite your grueling efforts to get them together, there's the danger that you actually come to develop a stake in their *not* being friendly to each other—because when *they* make up, you feel a little foolish for having gotten so embroiled in the first place. Besides, buffers never get thanks, only bruises (and usually from both sides). Try staying out of the next brawl. You may find that it doesn't last any longer or become any more angry or wild for *your* nonintervention, after all. Besides, unless you're planning to sit around there *indefinitely* as referee/peacemaker, you might as well stop playing that role for them now, and let the chips fall where they may. Is that heartless? No way; just smart.
- TAKE A LESSON. Try not to let your parents' conflicts sour you on marriage in general. *Yours* doesn't have to be anything like *theirs*. While it's certainly true that all couples have some problems, what you're learning now might help you avoid some of the kinds of mistakes your folks have been making. *At least* you will have the option of dealing

with the little problems and snaggles *as they come
up* instead of waiting until they've grown into deep
and habitual bitterness that spills out onto the kids.

Chapter 22: SPLITSVILLE! WAS IT YOUR DOING?

(Are you doomed to repeat? Is there any place for you to live?)

According to the Bureau of the Census, there are over three million fourteen- to seventeen-year-olds living with one parent; and 93 percent of that age group have experienced the upheaval of parental divorce. The trouble is, it's become *so* common, so run-of-the-mill and par-for-the-course, that many people forget how painful it can be when the *split-up parents are yours.*

Oh, sure. People do still worry *some* about the *young* child of divorce, but little, if any, attention is paid to the young adult whose parents divorce.

If they are your parents, chances are you're in for a lonely, complicated, and unexpectedly intense experience. Parents may be so wrapped up in their own emotional and financial problems that they may seem to forget all about their grown children, perhaps not bothering to explain much of anything. If they are aware of their children, it may be more to lean on them than support the son's or daughter's sagging spirits. This can be quite draining, especially if the mother or father implies that his or her future happiness is in the child's hands.

What can make it doubly hard is not only having to deal with the present effects of the split, but having to work through the cumulative stress of all those years the parents were together slugging it out—or worse, suffering in ominous silence.

Young-adult offspring of divorce who feel as if they are "going rather crazy" and want to be cradled in someone's arms may find some comfort in knowing that such anxiety is not unusual. If you're over sixteen or seventeen, people don't give you nearly so much credit for suffering a crisis as you deserve. But it *is* a crisis, and like other crises, it can go either of two ways. It can be an emotional rabbit punch, knocking you out for all future relationships, or it can lead to the development of unusual personal strength. We're firmly convinced that your ability and willingness to understand your feelings may make a good outcome more likely.

The Ostrich Defense.

Take Sandy, for example. At nineteen, she was clearly a victim of the ostrich syndrome.

"When parents of friends got divorced, we'd gossip about it and say we felt so sorry for the kids, but it was a smug, malicious sort of pity, because we knew that nice people didn't do that sort of thing."

So it was more than a little disconcerting when, in the middle of her sophomore year in college, Sandy's father moved out of the family's comfortable house. "There were no histrionics when he left; the whole thing reeked of unhappiness and rejection and fear and bitterness, but it was all very . . . polite." That was characteristic of the family, in which, Sandy said, there was never any fighting or arguing.

"I felt sorry for my mother," she says, "but my sympathy was laced with scorn. I thought she'd lost him because of her refusal to fight with him or for him. Perhaps they're the same thing. I vowed that I'd never let what happened to her happen to me. I'd also never be totally dependent on a man for my happiness, and I'd never let myself be an underdog.

"Of course, I was terribly unfair. After all, she was being very brave, very resilient, refusing to lean on any of us kids."

As for Sandy's father ("an attractive, easygoing guy who was away on business a good deal, but loved us in his own way"), "I was furious—I knew perfectly well he wasn't just divorcing a wife. He was walking out on the whole family—the noise and clutter and blaring records and curlers at the dinner table. It was a farce, and I resented it when he suddenly turned into Superdad right after the divorce. He was showing interest in us to try to ease his conscience, and maybe it fooled the younger kids, but not me."

Sandy did not avoid her father, but found it a strain to spend time with him. "He said he enjoyed my adult companionship, but I was still a child in his eyes. I couldn't give him advice or question anything, that was clear enough. But he wanted me to listen to his loneliness. He'd put on this big show of confiding. He'd say, 'Your mother and I were both good people, but the marriage has lost everything.' I tried hard to understand that concept—until it turned out that it had been a big lie. All the time there'd been another woman in the picture, and there I'd been—dutifully trying to understand his grandiose, phony soul-searching.

"Still, in spite of that, it seemed sad for him, eating frozen egg rolls for dinner, and taking his little plastic basket of laundry down to the basement. He seemed so pathetic."

It was natural enough for Sandy to be angry at her father—just as it was understandable that she might feel vicariously threatened by her *mother's* humiliation. But since she had been raised in an atmosphere of enforced tranquility, Sandy was very quick to hedge those unac-

ceptable gut reactions—for which she paid a price. "I was so depressed for a long while that I couldn't make myself cook or even take a bath. I'd think, 'What's the point?' "

One recent psychological study shows that children who claim they didn't know there was trouble between their parents "suffered more than those who admitted to sensing that separation was on the way. These innocents were only reflecting the extent to which they were encouraged by their parents to deny everything their senses told them was the true situation."

"Sandy's situation," says Dr. Lee Salk, Director of the Division of Pediatric Psychology at the New York Hospital-Cornell Medical Center, and author of *Preparing for Parenthood* "reflects a whole suburban syndrome: it's precisely this kind of homogenized community with only token acceptance of differences and great pressure to conform to a fictionalized 'everything's perfect' image, that leads to the degeneration of the family. If everything hadn't been so determinedly pleasant on the surface, Sandy might have been aware of the tension between her parents; the split would have been less shocking, and would have given Sandy some justification for her own negative feelings towards her parents, which make her feel guilty."

For an adult (or near-adult) child of divorce, as well as for a younger one, it's very hard to avoid some sense of guilt or responsibility. It's also not unusual in a case like this to feel betrayed when parents reveal they're separating. If their whole example of love for each other was a sham, maybe they didn't love the child much, either.

While grown children do not usually imagine, as young children often do, that they somehow came between their parents and *caused* the divorce, they may erroneously feel another kind of personal responsibility with at least as much guilt attached, which might be expressed as: "If they've been holding their breath waiting for me to grow up so they could split with a clear conscience, then I'm to blame for keeping them trapped all these years, and I don't see how I can ever make it up to them."

Guilty?

"Guilt," says Dr. Salk, "can be such an all-pervasive feeling that any transition in life can cause it: death, the end of a friendship. Whether they feel that they caused the divorce—*or* caused their parents to stay together unhappily—most children may feel some guilt."

Being aware of guilt, among all the other confusing reactions, can relieve some of the unhappiness and clear up some of the realities of the situation. As hard as it was for Sandy, *the divorce did give her an opportunity to see each parent as an individual,* rather than part of a

mythically happy family unit, and this made Sandy
think deeply for the first time about her own role as a
woman, and about what she herself needed to accomplish in order to be happy.

Martin: a sense of loss.

A feeling of powerlessness and abandonment can be
at least as distressing as guilt. Martin's parents' marriage had always been dismal; and so his first reaction to
the news of the split was calm approval. But then, he
panicked.

Even though he had been living with an older,
graduate-student girlfriend in her apartment, Martin
suddenly felt homeless. His mother and father had sold
their house and moved to small apartments, neither of
which had even a daybed set aside for Martin's use.
Their altered financial situation meant that there would
be virtually nothing for Martin to fall back on if he
wanted to quit college (where he had a scholarship and
a campus job). Martin's father did not even send him a
birthday card the first year. But Martin felt too broken
up to acknowledge how much it hurt him not to have a
caring father in the picture; instead, he talked about *his*
obligations to his father. "How can I just brush my
father off?" he asked his friends, as though he, and not
his father, were doing the rejecting.

According to Dr. Salk, "Martin was able to acknowledge the extent of his parents' discord, but he hadn't
come to terms with his father's lack of interest in him.
Since what happens in a divorce usually mirrors what's
happened earlier, Martin's problems probably related
less to the divorce itself than to the situation that prevailed during his childhood." Dr. Salk feels that some
professional counseling is a good idea if feelings of rejection cause a deep depression or severe panic.

Eve: a wall of defenses.

Often, an adult child's own love and sex life can be painfully vulnerable to unresolved feelings about the parents' relationship. Eve "ran the whole gamut" after her parents parted acrimoniously when she was seventeen.

"First, I said I'd never get married; I wasn't going to get mired in anything permanent. I became involved with several men. When my mother wasn't dating, I felt guilty for having men friends and a source of affection, but when she found someone to date, it made me very uptight. I was afraid to trust a man, afraid of caring.

"By the time I was finally able to admit that I wanted a relationship, I'd lost all confidence that I'd be able to recognize or attract a good man—after all, look how my mother messed up—so I began to search for Mr. Right in a very cerebral, methodical way, avoiding anyone who was anything like my father. I was so afraid of any sign of instability in a man that I'd overreact and only go for the type who seemed super-stable.

"Now I feel I've done enough thinking to know what I want. I don't want to get overconfident though, because I'm still at the point where it shocks me to see a married couple who really like and respect each other."

Dr. Salk feels that, "Eve had gone through so much thinking and analyzing that she's over-contrived; she's figured everything out intellectually, but she has very little awareness of her *feelings*." He says that Eve's overconsciousness of her actions may be her way of fending off the love that she wants, but either fears or believes that she doesn't deserve.

Alex: "A real relief."

Some parents' divorces, however, make their adult or near-adult children actually feel better, not worse.

YOU MEAN **YOUR** PARENTS REALLY LIKE EACH OTHER ?

Should they feel guilty about that? No, says Dr. Salk. Some people are, remarkably, broadened and strengthened. Alex, whose parents didn't part until he was twenty, had been quite aware of their misery. When he was little, his Hulk and Superman dolls were "friends of Mommy," never Daddy's; and when he was prevailed on to play "wedding" with neighborhood children, "something tragic would always happen to the groom."

Instead of making him bitter, however, a childhood of living within a bad marriage forced Alex to develop so strong a commitment to his own emotional survival that, when his parents did divorce, he was able to resist all his mother's tearful attempts to get him to stay at home. Alex went to law school and did so well that he had his pick of jobs when he graduated.

While someone with such a jaded view of domesticity might have been expected to flee from marriage, or to search vainly for some idealized mate, Alex's marriage is based on mutual trust and respect, the kind of relationship many people would enjoy.

According to Dr. Salk, *some people are weakened, even immobilized by stress; others are apparently invigorated.* "In spite of the conditions in Alex's family, it is more than likely that one or both of his parents gave him enough of a feeling of self-esteem in the critical first years of life for him to have developed the emotional strength to cope as he did."

Doomed to repeat?

It is natural enough to worry about divorce as a sort of hereditary disease. Sally is married and the mother of a three-year-old. She took it in stride when last year— apparently out of the blue—her parents separated. Now, however, she is deeply concerned: is *she* more likely to get divorced because her parents split? And what about her daughter's future prospects and general mental health?

"One possible reaction to parental divorce," says Dr. Salk, "is an exaggerated amount of vigilance and determination to 'succeed' in one's own marriage." But he feels that one can't forecast the success of anyone's marriage by the presence or absence of a parental divorce; the kind of relationship the parents had when the child was young is what matters.

One element of a successful marriage is how much we learned to like and trust the opposite sex when we were children. This may not be so much a matter of how objectively "good" each parent was. If, for example, the father was a solid type, but, at a critical age, the mother instilled in the child a feeling that the father was untrustworthy, the child might tend, in his or her own marriage, to fear closeness or, perhaps, to cling excessively.

Dr. Salk feels that, in any case, *"We must stop looking at divorce as a sign of failure;* it can be a sign of

success when it's warranted; there are many marriages that haven't ended in divorce that should have." And he says that he has run into as many people who wish that their parents *had* divorced as people who wish that their parents had not. He points out that children of divorce aren't necessarily the most anxiety-ridden about "failing." "Someone whose parents divorced might have a calm, tolerant attitude towards divorce as a solution, while someone else with no divorce in the family, but a very strong religious orientation, might feel that divorce not only means failing in life, but roasting in hell as well."

No question, it's a *big* emotional upheaval when your parents split—no matter how old and established you are, no matter how many of your friends have already gone through it. No, you certainly don't have to repeat your parents' pattern, as long as you realize that harmony in marriage is to be achieved not by the absence of problems, but by a mutual willingness to deal with them —even if doing so would make a lot of waves.

DESERTED!

While joint custody is increasingly popular these days, we all know that there are many situations in which one parent simply takes off and disappears. And when the defection is so clear and obvious, the remaining parent can't even offer you the good consolation prize that "even if you can't have both your parents together, at least you can have them both separately, both available to you."

What's tough, and also extremely important, to keep in mind is that your parent left for his/her *own* troubled reasons. You may be "sure" that you were bad or unlovable; that you hated him/her too much—or didn't love him/her enough. Wishing and hating *didn't* make it happen. You didn't drive him/her away; and there wasn't a thing you should have done or could have done to make him/her stay. IT IS VERY SAD THAT HE/SHE COULDN'T STAY AROUND TO BE A PARENT TO YOU. Your loss? For sure! Your fault? **No way.**

Chapter 23: A "REPLACEMENT-PART" PARENT? WHO NEEDS IT?

(Adjusting to a stepparent.)

Being a stepchild used to be good for lots of sympathy, if not some morbid curiosity, on the part of friends and acquaintances. But the grim Cinderella scenario is finally changing. It's about time, too, for the stepfamily has long deserved a better image—especially now that so many people are living in one.

But to say that all "recycled" families are happy is just replacing a bad myth with an equally untrue good one. For no amount of sugar-coating can disguise the resentment, confusion, territorial battles, power struggles, and hurt feelings that are inevitable in the real-life adjustment of even the very nicest steppeople.

If you or one of your friends has experienced it, then you know that no matter how good all the people are—and how much everyone wants it to work—settling into a new family can be painful.

John, a Mobile, Alabama, high school sophomore, has this to say: "The new arrangement doesn't just quietly enlarge your family, filling in the empty spaces; it's demolishing the family scene you're used to and rebuilding a whole new unfamiliar one." A blended family combines two different backgrounds and personalities (the parents') and then adds children: his, hers, or both. All of this, says Bismark, North Dakota, family counselor Marietta Eckberg, results in conflict and disorientation, and plenty of it.

Your demifamily may have been lonely before, but now that it's presumed to be "complete," you are assaulted with new rules and roles, new people—and a new feeling of rootlessness. Take Liz, for example: she had just made the swimming team and was up for student council vice-president and head cheerleader, when her mother remarried—and took Liz away from the school, the neighborhood, and the house that had been "real security blankets" in her life so far. Or consider Parker, an only child of sixteen, who thought it would be fun to acquire a brother when his mother remarried—until he found his private world and orderly life-style irrevocably shattered by his boisterous, demanding new brother, Patrick.

Not that Liz or Parker couldn't meet the challenge and even derive personal enrichment from having done so. But it's not much fun at the time you're going through the adjustment. Often, there are other, less clear-cut losses in store for the young person whose father or mother is remarrying.

Kate: second thoughts.

Kate, for example, was pleased when her mother, after six years of widowhood, began to see Frank, an old family acquaintance. Now that her mother had a social life, Kate figured, she could enjoy her own dates without any twinge of guilt about her mother being lonely. It was also cheering to see that "even with wrinkles and gray hair, a woman can be attractive." But months later, when her mother and Frank announced their engagement, Kate's early warm acceptance of Frank turned to intense dislike. "He's scrawny," she told a friend. "And his teeth look like he never brushes them."

Perhaps Kate's turnabout was a kind of double-take, a delayed realization that Frank was moving in on what had been her father's territory. When a father has departed, through death or the divorce court, it's not at all unnatural to feel that other men who come along are interlopers. A college dean from Michigan who married a widower with two teenage daughters calls it the mommies-and-daddies-are-made-in-Heaven syndrome. **It can happen with kids of any age, she says, "Though it's less intense when the stepchild is old enough to have already started dating and to understand it's possible to like more than one person."**

Moreover, a guy with yellow teeth—no matter how decent he is or how much Kate's mother may care for him—is simply not the John Wayne type Kate might have had in mind for a stepfather. And the longer the time between the departure of a parent and the arrival of a stepparent, the harder it is to trade in fantasy ideas for a warts-and-all human being.

S-E-X.

Here's something else: no matter how sophisticated and enlightened we are, it's difficult to feel comfortable about the obvious sexuality implied in a parent's impending marriage. For this reason, many young people will view a parent's prospective remarriage as "alarming, unsettling, frightening," says Anne W. Simon, author of *Stepchild in the Family: A View of Children in Remarriage.* This idea was illustrated in a TV play a while back in which acress Linda Blair lashed out at her stepfather: **"You're not my father. You're just the person who sleeps with my mother!"**

It takes a good deal of compassion and maturity to overcome the embarrassment and general discomfort of the situation.

> If the new stepfather seemed all right before you knew he was going to become the new stepfather, chances are he's still all right.

The goal is to try and accept him not as the Brave New Dad you'd secretly wished for, but as the man your mother has decided she'd like to share the rest of her life with, starting now—and continuing later, after you're launched on a life of your own.

Marcy: a loss of territory.

Sometimes the problems don't surface until the new family is united. Marcy, a senior at a high school outside of Denver, was overjoyed that her father had decided to marry Jean. As a matter of fact, it was Marcy who had introduced them when she was a candy striper at the hospital where Jean was an emergency room nurse.

But all too soon, the family honeymoon was over. Instead of being an older friend and new young mother, Marcy thought Jean was coming on as "an intruder and a prude." Dates on school nights, curlers and TV at the dinner table were early casualties of the new regime. Also, where Marcy had once been queen of the kitchen, she now found herself unceremoniously demoted to carrot-scraping and table-setting.

Things got more and more oppressive. Marcy's spontaneous gin rummy games with her father were crowded out by his need for time alone with Jean. As for the happily anticipated woman-to-woman talks between Marcy and Jean, they never got off the ground. Whenever Marcy tried to get into one, Jean was too busy.

Not only was Jean usurping Marcy's prerogatives, freedom, and claim on her father's free time, but also she was failing to provide what sociologists call "the benefits and warmth of a mother person in the house."

In fact, even though she was in a motherly sort of profession, Jean was far from an instant pro as a mother. Even her good deeds had a way of misfiring. For example, Jean had secretly worked for weeks on a new bedspread, dressing-table skirt, and curtains for Marcy's room. Even though everything was just the style and fabric Marcy would have picked out herself, she resented Jean's doing it *to* her instead of in consultation *with* her.

To Marcy, it was just another example of Jean's pushiness; to Jean, it was an incomprehensible rejection and another symbol of her evident failure in her new role.

"Most stepparents," says Helen Thomson, author of *The Successful Stepparent,* "are weighted down by a lot of unrealistic notions about what goes on in other people's families. They torture themselves with their convictions that other people's children do their chores

. . . and never act self-centered or sassy." This, of course, puts more pressure on the stepmother, who may be just a bit jealous of the first marriage, fearful of how she's shaping up in comparison with wife number one, and uptight about how her husband rates her amateur mothering skills. And all that is particularly likely, if, as with Jean, the new wife has never been married before. You can bet that none of it makes for peace.

As Anne Simon says: "There is a kernel of truth in the stepmother fiction. To some degree, a stepmother *is* jealous, hostile, competitive and at times, even cruel toward her husband's children; they are all this and more toward her. She *does* intrude on their relationship with their father; equally, they intrude on her marriage to him." A rather striking thought when you consider that there's always the possibility of ending up in the same boat someday—meeting and falling in love with some wonderful man with a daughter who may find *you* infuriatingly slow to learn the ropes.

The sibling complications.

Even in their original families, brothers and sisters are not famous for getting along with one another. Nor does it automatically iron out in adulthood, as everyone says it will. So why on earth should you and your stepparent's children fit together with perfect harmony? It can happen, but it's not so very likely.

What's more common is hot-and-cold-running hostility. "There is no more disunited a nation," says Anne Simon, "than the stepfamily which assembles his and her children under one roof." Certainly, on top of a natural guardedness and suspicion between the kids on the bride's side and those on the groom's side, there are bound to be skirmishes over literal and figurative territory. There is suddenly a lot more competition for the bathtub, the phone, and the portable TV. Maybe the going-to-college money has to be spread a lot thinner. And the parents themselves (plus their time and their enthusiasm) can be stretched only so far. ("Hey, that's *my* father taking *her* son horseback-riding.")

If you were an only child before, you may find yourself tossed for the first time into competition. We know one boy, for example, who gained ten pounds under the pressure of acquiring a stepsister the same age who was a better student, had a better batting average, and played the trombone—beautifully. Even if you have had siblings of your own before, you may be losing your distinct, established position as, say, the oldest in the family, or the only girl—or something specialized like the "family comic" or "the artistic one." That may require a complete reorganization in the way you relate to people outside the family as well.

On the plus side.

There are some—honestly. A stepsibling can eventually turn out to be a good friend or welcome ally with you against both your respective parents—or at least another warm body in the family to deflect some of the intense feelings away from *your* back.

Even if none of the above apply, and your stepbrother or stepsister is absolutely awful, you have the consolations that (1) he or she may improve and (2) he or she may have the same irritating, but ultimately beneficial effect on your life as a grain of sand in an oyster's shell. Instead of a pearl in your case, you're developing, perforce, a lifetime supply of poise and ingenuity in dealing with difficult people. And that will take you far.

While no sane person would set out to acquire a stepfamily for the sake of the maturity to be gained from the experience, it's one good by-product you can count on. The important thing is not to avoid or deny the problems and bad feelings. The ability to acknowledge and work with what you are feeling is well worth striving for. It's the best way to discover that with all the changes, the aches, the rearrangements, and the readjustments, you're still you, after all.

NOBODY WANTS ME.

Sometimes a marriage can be so stormy and troubled that you:

- get lost in the struggling, or . . .
- become, for each parent, a symbol of their pain and a scapegoat for the real and imagined "crimes" of the other parent.

Then, whether they stay together or not, you feel that you don't belong and aren't wanted— by either of them.

No matter how bad things get at home, no matter how tempted you may be to take off, don't do it on impulse. You can't imagine the kinds of people who regularly haunt the highways and bus stations just to prey on young runaways. If you feel that you can't stay at home, and that you have no place to go, call the National Runaway Switchboard (toll-free, 800-621-4000). They can offer you help at any hour of the day or night. They can refer you to a safe, temporary refuge for a few days' lodging, comfort, and counseling.

If it turns out that neither parent is able to make a home for you, a trained counselor will be able to suggest a foster family or supervised adolescent group home, sponsored by a social or religious organization, WHERE YOU WILL NOT BE ALONE OR UNWANTED.

Reaching out.

If you feel—or have been feeling—down about your parents' divorce, you may want to look into the International Youth Council (IYC), which is the teen division of the well-known support group, Parents Without Partners.

With over 100 chapters, IYC brings young people together to share ideas and companionship in a very constructive way. Panel discussions and talks on discipline, drugs, alcohol, getting along with parents, dating, money, and other topics are lively and useful.

Not that IYC is all work and no play. One IYC chapter planned a night-owl bus ride, visiting police stations, hospitals, and night court—followed by breakfast at a favorite spot. Another group put on a carnival at a children's hospital, complete with games and refreshments.

If you'd like to find out where the closest IYC chapter is, look up Parents Without Partners in your phone book; or, call (toll-free) 800-638-8078; or write: Information Center, Parents Without Partners, Inc., 7910 Woodmont Avenue, Washington, DC 20814.

(P.S. It's not necessary for your parent to belong to Parents Without Partners for you to become a member of IYC. Any young person from twelve through seventeen may join IYC if their parents are separated, divorced, widowed, or never married.)

Chapter 24: WHEN ONE OF YOUR PARENTS IS DYING

(Helping yourself and the other members of your family get through it.)

When Margaret's father had a serious heart attack, her mother was adamant about protecting him from the knowledge that he was probably going to die. "I know what he can take and what he can't," she said. "He'd definitely go to pieces if he knew." Margaret, on the other hand, remembered certain conversations years ago in which her father had said that he'd want to know if he were dying, because he'd hate to be made a fool of by other people knowing and lying to him.

Depressed and confused, Margaret found excuse after excuse to stay away from the hospital. She didn't know how to behave with her father: she was terrified of doing the "wrong" thing, and also scared of facing him undecided. As it happened, he went into a coma before she got to see him, and he never came out of it. Margaret now wishes she had been able to make up her mind. She can't help feeling that she let her father down.

To tell or not to tell.

It is a mistake, psychotherapists say, to get hung up on the issue of whether to tell a person he's dying—or even of how to tell him. If you can be quiet and perceptive, says one New York doctor, you never need to make a blunt announcement—he'll tell you! Sometimes just asking him how he feels—without adding hurriedly that

143

he *looks* great, or that the new medicine will probably do wonders—will be just the opening he's longed for. He may tell you he's scared, or he may cry, and you might find yourself clutching each other and crying together. Death per se, may not come up, but a lot can be said without a speech, without any words.

Most therapists, social workers, and "death counselors" stress the fact that insisting a person be frank in discussing his own impending death is dogmatic and pointless, as well as unkind. (Some people can; some cannot.) The aim is simply to make dying a little easier; to offer the option for it to be an intimate, rather than a solitary experience.

Swiss psychiatrist Dr. Elisabeth Kubler-Ross has found that even the most mature and philosophical patient only *gradually* comes to accept his or her approaching death—usually in a set of distinct phases.

- First there's disbelief or denial: a mood of this can't be happening to *me*.
- The next is anger—the furious realization that it's no mistake or mixed-up X-rays after all, but *why me?*
- The third stage is an attempt at bargaining or making a deal with death ("I'll be docile and uncomplaining if I can have just a little more time. . .").
- The fourth stage is a deep depression in which the patient mourns for what he's already suffered, and grieves the loss of everything and everyone he loves. And, if he hasn't been distracted from his task and held back by the people trying to "cheer him up," he'll transcend his pain and despair and arrive at—
- the fifth and final stage: a fearless, resolved, and panic-free acceptance of death.

Each person is unique and the stages are rarely en-

tered in a neat, consecutive order. The anger and the depression, for example, can alternate, only to be followed by another attempt at bargaining. Or one stage could be skipped or never reached. At any rate, a person's progress through the phases is his own—and all the more reason for the family to avoid trying to do the pacing for him.

Frustration!

You, as the son or daughter, will at times feel frustrated and helpless, but many of the seemingly illogical concerns of a dying person will make sense if they are understood in terms of the phase he is going through.

Take Barry, for example. When his father was hospitalized for a third and final time with a malignant tumor, Barry couldn't understand his father's intense concern over such "trivia" as the floor nurse's trouble placing a litter of puppies. "Why does he care so much,"

Barry wondered, when he arrived at his father's bedside to find him phoning all his friends in an exhausting search for homes for the dogs. It was as if Barry (who had put aside *everything* to be with his father) wasn't even there.

The next day, Barry was even more distressed. When he arrived at the hospital, he found his father on the phone with his travel agent, getting information on skin-diving spots in the Caribbean—for an intern who had mentioned that he had a vacation coming up.

What Barry didn't realize—and had no way of knowing—was that his father was doing what was important to him at that time. In part, he may unconsciously have been trying to "bribe his captors" (members of the hospital staff) with favors in exchange for a "reprieve," a new lease on life. But Barry's father was doing something else in making those phone calls from what was, indeed, to be his deathbed: he was exercising his last chance to be a benefactor, a provider, a big shot, before succumbing to the humiliation of his rapidly advancing helplessness.

For dignity's sake.

Just because a person is aware that he hasn't long to live doesn't mean that he's going to lie in bed and let all his prerogatives slip away without a fight. It's worth doing all you can to help him keep that dignity intact. And that might include speaking out and asking an insensitive nurse (or relative or anybody) to stop talking baby-talk to your mother or father, just because she or he is unable to eat or talk, or has wasted away to child-size. EVEN WHEN A PERSON IS IN A COMA AND SEEMS TO BE TOTALLY OBLIVIOUS, HE MAY BE ABLE TO SEE OR HEAR, BUT BE INCAPABLE OF RESPONDING.

Future-shock?

If the dying parent is articulate and able to assert himself, he may find it emotionally rewarding to actually make the practical preparations for his approaching death. Many people do. If your mother, for example, wants to talk about the details of her funeral, the way someone else would plan a wedding, don't just tell her that she's being morbid or silly. She isn't.

Apart from discussing the events that will actually concern the dying parent, you feel uncomfortable or embarrassed about talking of the future; it's all too obvious that *he'll* be dead and you'll be alive.

You may be tempted to try to reassure a dying parent how bleak your world will be when he is gone; and he may even, especially at first, seem to be asking for that very reassurance. In any case, there's no need to avoid talking about the future.

Some dying people are eager to participate in planning for the real future of those they care about or feel responsible for. John Hinton, a British psychiatrist, says that the dying person "is normally immensely concerned over the family he is about to leave. He will want to know, preferably directly from them, that they are self-supporting, or that someone has adequately taken over both small and great duties that he thought essential. If they seem secure, then the dying person is less troubled." He *still* wants to feel connected with them.

Something to hold onto.

This can extend in many directions. It can be as pragmatic as seeing to it that anyone who works for him will have a definite job to go to. It can be as selfless as urging his wife to marry again. It can be quiet, joyous moments of holding a daughter's hand and sharing her dreams of a future marriage and career.

Or it can be the sort of thing that Joan's father did. Although they'd been on good terms up until the time he got sick, they hadn't been especially close. Joan, a college senior, was rather taken aback when he asked her point-blank if there was a man in her life, if he was single, and if she would mind asking him to come up to the hospital some evening to meet him.

Joan certainly had some trepidation about the whole thing. First of all, the relationship was young and hadn't nearly gotten to any come-meet-the-parents stage. But she did call her boyfriend who (miraculously) wasn't scared off. When he arrived, Joan's father was jovial and relaxed. He explained all about his illness—what had happened so far and what was expected, and said, "Look, I know you're probably wondering what the hell you are doing here now. I love Joan a lot and since I probably won't have the pleasure of meeting her husband, I thought it would be nice to see what kind of guy she's interested in these days. I don't know what your relationship is—you might be friends or you might break up tomorrow, and it's none of my business. All I can say is that just meeting you, I can tell she's got sense and I feel one hell of a lot better."

The tone of the visit was light and full of good feeling, which was what Joan remembered in the months that followed, because as her father's disease wore on, his good humor and concern gave way to impatience, bursts of temper, and long, cold silences.

It's the kind of thing that she never expected, especially since their relationship had grown closer. But it happens frequently: getting jealous of the "survivors," resenting their robust good health and strength.

This hostility can take the form of rage or heavy sarcasm, accusations, a barrage of unreasonable criticism or a tearful, self-righteous insistence that nobody cares. It can be grueling *for you,* but it rarely goes on for very long. An understanding that it *can* happen is some help in rallying the strength, compassion, and confidence needed to cope.

Sharing.

Fortunately, in most cases, the death of a parent doesn't have to be faced alone. There's still the other parent or at least a close aunt or uncle, brother or sister, or husband to help absorb some of the emotional high-voltage of the situation.

Sometimes the shared crisis gives a brother and sister the opportunity and incentive to get to know and like each other better. It may create an illusion of a Whole New Relationship, making things easier and nicer for the time being—even if, after the crisis is over, the relationship erupts into petty fighting about who gets a box of tattered old photos and who gets the "better" of two nearly identical bracelets. That, too, passes, and the *net* result may be a somewhat better relationship.

Helping the rest of the family.

Young children in the family or the widowed parent tend to be the ones who suffer most from the death. Maybe you are in a position to help them.

Children under twelve may be plagued with guilt and worries beyond anything you feel. They may not look or act particularly distraught, but the chances are they're worrying plenty: not only about whether they'll be adequately cared for after the parent dies, but also about whether they'll have to start taking care of the other parent.

They are also less able than you are to acknowledge and understand that mixed with their sorrow is anger at the dying parent for deserting the family. Maybe the feeling of relief that "at least now Mom will never be able to yell at me again." This makes for guilt . . . to the point where very young children may even feel, sometimes unconsciously, that they are responsible for the death.

Dr. Morris A. Wessel, an associate professor of pediatrics at the Yale School of Medicine in New Haven, Connecticut, says, "When sad feelings are so intense and anxiety-producing as to become unbearable, adolescents are likely to adopt a 'happy-go-lucky' frame of mind and an attitude of euphoria predominates. This 'short sadness span' . . . is difficult for adults to understand and accept."

It is important to realize the intensity of what they're going through, Dr. Wessel says. If young David would rather see a movie or play baseball with his friends than go to the hospital for a visit, he's not being disrespectful, necessarily. Curtailment of usual social life interferes with the need to deny the situation. It would give credence to the death—the very thing that he is attempting to deny. The overwhelming helplessness that arises when younger brothers and sisters allow themselves to think of what the loss of a parent really means is too big a burden to bear alone.

Just as the dying parent needs time to adjust, so does the younger child. Sometimes, the sad feeling will come out in unexpected ways: a seemingly callous little sister begins to weep uncontrollably over a sad episode in a TV serial that she's always made fun of in the past. She needs the same tactful, sensitive, open ear from an older sister or brother that the dying parent does.

Still, this understanding mustn't be forced. You may be tempted to try to be an extra parent to a younger brother or sister—only to find yourself unceremoniously rebuffed. The kid has probably idealized the parent he or she is about to lose into a superhero; and mentally comparing that paragon with you—the older brother or sister (clay feet and all)—finds *you* sorely lacking as a substitute. Your best bet: to let them know, in a low-key way, that you are there and available. Period.

Helping the other parent.

With a parent who's about to become a widow or widower, the problems are quite different. Dr. Wessel says that there is a tendency on the part of grown children to "try to make everything all right again" by filling in as many of the dying parent's roles and functions as possible. While it may be very helpful to fill in *specific* gaps (such as cooking a meal or several; getting neglected repairs done; arranging or providing lodging for visiting relatives), Dr. Wessel cautions against being so accommodating that you sacrifice your own freedom. Don't!

If, for example, you've moved into a college dorm, it would be a mistake to move back. That could create dependency on you and a pattern of expectation that can be hard to break, even a long time later. **The aim is not to try to replace the parent who is going to die, but to make life (and the other parent's adjustment to widowhood) a bit easier.**

It takes a lot of personal judgment to know when to offer comfort and solace—and when to administer a dose of something stronger. For example, when Olivia's father was dying, Olivia could see that her mother was somehow managing to insulate herself against the reality of what was going to happen.

One night, as the two women left the hospital together, Olivia suggested a more leisurely dinner than their usual quick hamburger. Over coffee, Olivia gently asked her mother such things as, "Was she going to sell the house afterward? Would she need or want to find a full-time job? Would she be going out to California for a while to stay with her married daughter?"

Olivia's frankness in presenting the necessity of thinking seriously about those things was a help. Her mother found that it was something of a relief to finally quit denying that she would soon be a widow. She was then able to make more fruitful use of the remaining time she still had with her husband, and to consult with him on the matters that concerned her future. When she made changes, they were the result of *considered* decisions rather than confused ones.

By the end of the meal, both women were crying. It can be a great relief, and consolation, when a mother and daughter (or father and son)—each of them wanting to "be strong" for the other one—can cry together.

In the long run, considering the terrible isolation in death that our society fosters with its stoic taboo on the show of emotion, and its sterile segregation of the dying in hospitals and nursing homes, feelings shared are the strongest, and perhaps the only, weapon we have.

If you are losing, or have recently lost, one of your parents, there are people specially trained to offer you the kind of counseling and comfort you could use at this point.

If your parent is or has been in a hospital, ask to talk to the social worker there. If not, try your phone book for "mental health center" or "hotline." Either one ought to be able to steer you towards a good, local source of bereavement counseling or a support group for the terminally ill and their families.

Chapter 25: EMBARRASSING COMPLICATIONS

(A Mental Illness . . .)

"My mother is depressed. Not just sad, I mean she sits in a chair all day and only sighs. She stays in a nightgown and never combs her hair or takes a bath. She won't talk to me—or anyone. There's no way I can help her; she doesn't react when I smile or kiss her or squeeze her hand. Sometimes she moans and covers her face. It gives me the creeps when she does.

"My friends all have *normal* mothers. I hate feeling so different. When I'm out with my friends, I make up stories and pretend that my mother is just like theirs . . . I just hate the way things are. I don't understand. I don't even remember how she got this way—or when.

"Sometimes I think, if I only had a steady boyfriend, I wouldn't have to think about my mother so much . . . but I don't even date anyone. How *could* I ever let a boy into this house and see her?"

The speak-no-evil-syndrome.

A parent's mental illness might make you feel so embarrassed, so ashamed, that you don't discuss it—even with the other parent. Maybe the other parent is away a lot . . . or has other problems . . . or is just reticent to talk about what's going on. Then you end up feeling like that silence is a kind of rebuke—as if you are in some way responsible.

153

Let's say that the other parent isn't explaining anything about it. Maybe he/she even appears to be avoiding you for fear that you'll ask. So things are brisk and superficial and very strained.

Chances are, he/she is also having trouble dealing with the other parent's illness; and the well parent may be trying to "protect" you, on the loving, but erroneous, theory that the less he tells you about it, the less you'll suffer.

The trouble is, not talking about something tragic or threatening—like a parent's emotional illness—doesn't make it go away. "In the extreme," says therapist Ann Kliman, author of *Crisis,* and a director of the Center for Preventive Psychiatry, in White Plains, New York, "not talking about what's going on can actually be harmful." She goes on to describe an experiment that was done with the children of schizophrenic mothers: half the children were told nothing about their mothers' bizarre, explosive illness, while the other half were gently helped to understand that their mothers had a sickness and couldn't control their dress, their speech, their crazy-withdrawn or crazy-destructive behavior.

Years later, the results indicated that telling the children the reality not only didn't force them into the sick stuff, but also may well have been a factor in protecting them from developing the illness themselves. Talking appeared to be a major help, as many of the children who had been told nothing actually began to behave very much like their mothers had. Many of the other children (the ones who had been told, "Yes, it is scary and disappointing that Mother is sick and acts this way, but it is not your fault") says Dr. Kliman, "apparently did not have to feel responsible for their mothers' behavior, nor to identify with it, and so they didn't have to grow up schizophrenic."

The point is: no matter how well anyone means, keeping you uninformed doesn't protect you. **There is nothing too terrible to talk about.** At least if you talk about it, there is some hope of understanding. (So don't let yourself get caught up in *their* conspiracy of silence: you have a right to know. You need to know.)

- A PARENT'S MENTAL ILLNESS might make you feel super-obligated towards the other parent— as if it's *your* job to fill the gap. Actually it's most important that you *not* let your feelings of compassion—or obligation—carry you away to the extent that you give up your own activities and friends and fun. Don't let the painful situation at home keep you back.

- A PARENT'S MENTAL ILLNESS might make you fearful that you're in for the same thing some day. Most mental illness is *not* hereditary; but all you need to do is check with the family doctor (or another doctor) if you want to be sure of this.

- A PARENT'S MENTAL ILLNESS might make you feel isolated from your friends, afraid to let them know what's going on. Give them the benefit of the doubt: give them the opportunity of offering support and love. After all, you wouldn't be scornful of them if the shoe was on the other foot, would you? If your friend's parent suffered from a mental illness, you would feel good if your friend trusted you enough to talk, wouldn't you? And wouldn't you feel sad (and even annoyed?) if you felt that your friend had decided to avoid you or keep it a secret?

Chapter 26: ENDING IT ALL. THE PARENT WHO COMMITS SUICIDE

(And your survival.)

- *Lissa had been hunting for a summer job. When she got back from the city and called from the station for her mother to come and pick her up, a policeman answered the phone: Lissa's mother had taken an overdose of sleeping pills and was dead.*
- *Stan and his sister were visiting friends for the weekend when they got the word to come home right away: their father had put on a stack of records, locked the door, and hanged himself.*
- *Ginny's father had gone to a motel to shoot himself, fatally, in the head. His note explained that he'd "caused the family trouble enough as it is."*

Shocking cases, but not nearly so rare as you may think. Suicide is the sort of thing that happens more often than a lot of us realize, because, unless the facts absolutely can't be concealed "for public consumption," the story is told that so-and-so's parent died of natural causes. Does it seem more "respectable" for a parent to die in a one-car automobile crash than by his own gun or razor blade? Actually, some psychiatrists say that many "accidents" are deliberate or unconscious acts of suicide.

Is it really "kinder" or "easier" as far as the survivors are concerned to cover up, to pretend?

157

WELL, I DON'T THINK IT WAS **EXACTLY** A HEART ATTACK

Perhaps not.

Take Lissa, for example. Sure, she knew that her mother had been "sad." In fact, Lissa had joined her father in urging her mother to "go get some help," to see a doctor. Lissa also knew in her heart that all the love in the world *and* the best medical care can't keep a person alive against her will.

Still, perhaps because we live in a society in which the whole subject of suicide is still so shrouded in shame and an implicit sense of failure, if not liability, for the immediate survivors, Lissa could not bring herself to share her feelings with anyone. All she could do was repeat the "white lie" that her mother had suffered "heart failure." Period.

It was a savvy neighbor, however, who was also a trained pastoral counselor, who convinced Lissa that even if the rest of the family was intent on silence, Lissa could afford to cope with a more precise truth—i.e., that her mother had an emotional illness and died. In fact, her mother had been so desperately ill that she had felt she couldn't live with it and had stopped her life.

The neighbor encouraged Lissa to bare all her feelings of frustration and shock—and even anger for "doing it in spite of me and how much I loved her," by explaining that "part of your mother's sickness was that she couldn't really know that she was loved and she was needed."

"Look, Lissa," the neighbor/counselor said. "You are only seventeen. Your father is over forty and *he* couldn't stop your mom; and her doctor couldn't, and your grandmother Ethel couldn't. Sometimes a sickness is too extensive, too advanced even for loving and caring —and yes, even expertly trained—adults to prevent.

"Lissa, it is a tragedy that your mother couldn't know how much you and your family, and even her neighbors, wanted her to live. And, Lissa, it's sad that she wasn't able to talk about what she was feeling—like we can."

Help for survivors.

Lissa was fortunate in having someone so understanding to talk to. Not everyone in such a situation does. Recognizing the stresses and the isolation of almost anyone who has lost a parent (or any close relative or friend) to suicide, a group has formed in Cleveland, Ohio. Aptly, it is called "Survivors."

Survivors is a self-help group. It is for those who would like the comfort and understanding of others who have experienced a similar loss. It is dedicated to helping people survive the experience and move on.

"After a loss by death," says Survivors Director Morton November, "we go through several stages called grief reactions. Sometimes these stages unfold naturally and other times we get stuck in one stage or another. Following a death by suicide, the normal grief reactions are intensified, as there is no precedent for dealing with this experience."

November, who lost both his daughter and wife, says that survivors of a parent's or other close relative's suicide must cope with feelings of:

- emptiness.
- guilt.
- anger.
- despair.
- isolation.
- shame.
- depression.
- abandonment.
- helplessness.
- disorientation.
- stigma.
- disbelief.

Through monthly meetings (also attended by a social worker as consultant to the group), Survivors offers members help in coping with: anniversaries; holidays; memories; altered life-styles; explaining the death; getting through each hour and day; their own suicidal thoughts; feelings "we are not sure we should be having."

Survivors members help each other by: listening; accepting one another's rage, guilt, depression, self-centeredness, and blame without judging; letting them cry; not asking "Why?" as if there was anything that could have been done; realizing that mourning can take years and that the hurt is never forgotten.

If you want to write to Survivors to get in touch with them and find out about possibly starting your own local chapter, you can write to:

Survivors
c/o Suicide Prevention Center
10900 Carnegie Avenue, Room 410
Cleveland, OH 44106

They have a 24-hour phone number, which is 216-229-4545.

Chapter 27: THE PARENT WHO DRINKS

(Or, how not to get sucked in.)

If you have a parent with a drinking problem, the whole family—you included—must feel the effect. If you are like literally *millions* of other young people in the same boat, you have invested tremendous energy in trying to "solve" the problem, quietly, your own way—by:

- pretending the problem is just your imagination.
- pretending that it scarcely bothers you.
- threatening your parent (as in "I'll run away if you don't quit").
- offering deals (as in "I promise to get all A's" or "I promise to quit going out with so-and-so IF YOU'LL ONLY QUIT GETTING DRUNK!").
- taking it personally (as in trying to figure out what you've done or failed to do that's driving your parent to drink—or believing that if the drinking parent really loved you, he/she would stop drinking).
- avoiding friends for fear they'll see what's going on at home—and reject you.
- using the drinking as an excuse to be irresponsible—about school, about sex, about anything.
- putting life "on hold"; retreating into fantasy—as in "all things will be possible for me *after* my parent stops drinking; nothing will be possible for me until then."

Of course, the trouble is that none of these ploys really work. You're still left with all the pain and all the
original helplessness and anger—and the feeling that
you're all alone.

The one thing that *does* work, for most people, that is,
is something called "Alateen." Maybe you've heard of
it. Maybe you already know someone who goes.

- Alateen is a self-help program for young people
  who have been affected by someone else's drinking
  —most often it's a parent, sometimes both.
- Alateen is wherever you are. There are more than
  2000 groups meeting regularly; there is almost certain to be one near you. (If *not,* you can still get
  connected with them by correspondence.) Going to
  meetings is easy. There are no dues, only voluntary
  contributions; and when you go, you only tell your

first name. There will be one adult sponsor there, and the rest of the people are teenagers, like you.

How Alateen can get you off the hook.

One of the things Alateen does, according to a member named Irwin, is that "it allows you to detach yourself from your parent's drinking . . . so you don't have to feel responsible for it—or become a substitute parent, scolding or caring for the grown-ups."

Irwin says, "Most of us spent years trying to figure out *why* our parents were drinking—and how much, counting the empties in the trash, and how we could find some terrifically *creative* way to make them stop. In Alateen, I learned that *it doesn't matter why: what matters is how it affects our lives.*"

Susan, another Alateen member, agrees. "The point —for all of us—is that *we do* survive whether the parent stops drinking or not."

"We don't develop into super-humans," Irwin adds quickly. "I still get upset and scared by the drinking behavior. **But at least I don't sit around and wallow any more. I function.**"

Getting perspective.

"When your parents—or one parent—drinks," says Margo, another member, "it tends to dominate your life. I'm no Pollyanna; but in Alateen, I've found that my mother's drinking doesn't have to be the center of my universe. I have other, better, *pleasanter* things to think about. I don't have to sit there, biting my nails and suffering—at least not *all* the time." She smiles. "It's very nice," she says, "to be able to walk out of a crazy house and make the honor roll and the swim team, *in spite of what my parents are doing to themselves.*"

The other parent, the sober one—more trouble.

Alateen helps in another way, members say—that is, learning to cope with flack from the parent who isn't

drinking, who is ragged with frustration and disappointment and rage; who is, at least some of the time, unable
to keep from taking it out on you.

Alateen can also help you resist the impulse to try and
"make it up" to the nondrinking parent for what the
drinker is doing; and Alateen can help you stay neutral
and uninvolved in anything that's going on between the
two parents.

Happily ever after? Not so fast!

Even if your dream—that the drinking parent would
stop—comes true, there are plenty of feelings, not all of
them good, that can be shared with Alateen members so
that everybody benefits.

"I thought my dad's sobriety would make life
absolute heaven," Joyce, a two-year member of Alateen,
recalls. "But then there was this terrific letdown for me,
a feeling that nothing had changed after all. For instance, I was still afraid to speak up about anything—as
if the wrong word would set off the kind of drunken rage
I'd learned to dread. So I kept on walking on eggs, hiding my true feelings. If Dad was ten minutes late getting
home from work, I'd get the old sinking feeling, like,
'Oh, God. He's hitting the bars again.' When he *did*
come home sober and said he'd gotten caught in traffic,
I *still* felt mad as hell.

"He's been sober for a year now, but the tension, the
resentment still haven't gone away. When my brother
brought home a so-so report card and Dad said, 'How
come?' I felt like hitting the ceiling. I thought, 'Look at
the big shot. Trying to act like a father now, but where
was he two years ago when we were all so sad?'

"I'll tell you, I don't know how I'd manage without
the Alateen group. I can listen to people who've been
there before—who've had it all. It helps me stay sane, I

swear it does. Whatever I'm going through, I know I'm not alone."

A *"ticket in."*

It's a very hard thing to have a parent who drinks. Alateen has been described by one member as an entree, "a ticket in"—not only to get together with people who understand your problems and share your feelings, but also a ticket in to a very self-affirming, life-affirming point of view:

- to help you realize that you can't change anyone but you.
- to give you perspective so that if you do something wrong, you can forgive yourself and not have to dwell on it for weeks.
- to help you to form a constructive "how-can-I-change-to-improve-my-situation" approach to all kinds of *nonparent* problems in your life (including school, social life, getting along with difficult brothers or sisters, anything).

If you can't find Al-Anon or Alateen in your phone book, write to:

Al-Anon Family Group Headquarters
P.O. Box 182
Madison Square Garden
New York, NY 10159

Chapter 28: A PARENT IN JAIL

(It's real and it's no joke.)

It's something most of us never seriously think about, unless we happen to see an old James Cagney movie on TV. Otherwise, it's a vague concept of somewhere far away—a place where kiddie-porn sellers and muggers (when caught) and other "dregs of society" are stashed.

That was what Hilary, fifteen, thought—until her own handsome, well-dressed, college-educated father, with his church membership and his golf trophies, was sent to a large penitentiary for embezzling hundreds of thousands of dollars from the bank where he was an officer.

Hilary's mother, Ann. was "shocked, but not surprised" when the tragedy unfolded. Her husband hadn't told her what he'd been up to; but she knew the pressure he'd put himself under, the impossible money-making goals he'd set for himself—and his panic to maintain a life-style that was really beyond their means.

Ann was furious—and sad—but most of all, she was worried about Hilary. Hilary had always idolized her father. Ann toyed briefly with the idea of making up a story and telling Hilary that her father was going underground on a vital espionage mission for a couple of years. Something like that.

But after a sleepless night or two, Ann decided firmly that a fool's paradise was no place for her daughter.

169

When she sat Hilary down the next day and told her everything, Hilary kept shaking her head and saying, "No, no. I don't believe you." Then she burst into sobs that tore through Ann and made her angrier than ever at her husband's blind disregard for the consequences, *these* consequences of what he had done. Abruptly, Hilary stopped weeping and grabbed at the silver-framed photo of her father on the desk. She flung it savagely against the wall, smashing the glass into a thousand pieces.

While another mother might have said, "Yes, you're right, Hilary. Forget him," Ann sensed her daughter's continuing need—and love—for her father, despite Hilary's fierce insistence that, "He's a rotten crook and a liar and I never want to see him again."

Ann gradually was able to help Hilary pry herself out of the rigid and so very lonely right-is-right-and-wrong-is-wrong morality so typical of adolescents by reminding her that, "Nobody in the world is all good or all bad (and Hilary, you wouldn't be compromising *your* integrity if, say, you should decide that you want to write to your father sometime, or even go see him)."

Ann also reminded Hilary of the many sweet, loving, and responsible things about her father; and she helped in still another way. Hilary had taken to hanging around home an awful lot—avoiding school, where she had been involved in so many ways, and even avoiding her best friend. Not knowing quite how to put it at first, Ann finally stopped trying to make a speech and simply talked for hours with her daughter, somehow managing at last to make the important clarification for Hilary that, **"It is outrageous and maddening that Dad was so driven that he wasn't able to protect you from this. It will be hard on you when some of the kids at school find out, and some of the neighbors. You have every right to be**

furious and feel cheated and deprived by this. But you do not have to feel ashamed because you did not do it. You did not do anything wrong."

"Doing their time on the outside."

Even *with* a mother as wise and psychologically sophisticated as Hilary's, the experience of having a parent in jail can be an unimaginably lonely one. How can you help but wonder and worry over whether your parent will be irrevocably changed while he (or she) is away? Are jails as terrible as the newspapers say? (Will your parent be bullied, raped?)

What will you tell the snoopy people in town? And how do you act when they stare? Can you call your parent on the phone? How often?

What if the remaining-at-home parent can't keep up with mortgage payments and you have to move far away from all that's familiar?

What if the nonjailed parent is so mortified, confused, and seemingly helpless that you feel doubly deserted?

Fortunately, there is a group designed to help with all those problems and more. It's called Prison Families Anonymous, and it's located in Hempstead, Long Island, New York.

Like Alateen, almost everyone involved in PFA has now or at one time had someone in the family arrested, tried, or sentenced to prison; so members know what it feels like, what you're going through.

They say that you can benefit from the PFA Youth Program if:

- you have a parent who is or has been involved in the criminal justice system.
- you feel you could have done something to prevent your family member or friend from being taken away.
- you feel you got a rotten break in life.

- it's hard for you to talk to your family.
- you believe no one could possibly understand how you feel.
- you think everything will be better when your parent comes home.
- you find yourself doing things that get you into trouble.
- you cover up your real feelings by pretending you don't care.

Besides a regular program for adults, there is a youth program for people seventeen and under, who meet together every week to help one another deal with the painful and complicated feelings, as well as the practical problems, emanating from the fact of the situation.

MAYBE YOU WOULD LIKE TO GET IN-VOLVED IN SOMETHING LIKE THAT BUT LIVE TOO FAR AWAY. That's a problem, as the group is local at the moment; but it you'd like some literature, or information on how to contact members of PFA Youth Program, or get a similar group started near where you live, send a note with a self-addressed, stamped envelope to:

Prison Families Anonymous, Inc.
91 North Franklin Street
Room 304
Hempstead, NY 11550.

PFA assures us that your anonymity and confidentiality will be respected at all times.

Chapter 29: YOU DON'T HAVE TO FOLLOW IN THOSE FOOTSTEPS

If you've been through ANY OF THE ABOVE . . . .
It's reasonable to worry . . . .
   "Is this going to be my fate, too?"
   "Am I stuck in a pattern?"
   "Will I have no choice but to follow in the same sorry footsteps?"
It's true there is something called "repetition compulsion" that tends to make people repeat the very same tragic, hurtful, self-destructive behavior they saw in their parents. It can sneak up on you, too, as in the case of a young man, for example, who grows up hating liquor because his father is a drunk; but then slips into alcoholism himself—not at fifteen, not at eighteen, or even twenty-one, but at the age his father was when *he* (the son) became aware of his father's problem.

Still, the people who study this kind of thing are emphatic that the tendency to repeat **is in the head, not in the genes.** There **is** a good strategy for fighting it.

(1) FACE THE ISSUE. Be aware of what happened; don't pretend that everything was swell. Maybe it's easier to pretend and to avoid all the painful memories, but you really need to know if you want to put the shaky pieces back, in terms of

your own future—to go from helplessness to active coping.

(2) TALK IT OUT. *Don't let the hurt become a
permanent part of you,* like a wound or infection
that never really heals. It's only through bringing
these things to the surface and airing them that we
can experience the loss, the cruelty, the deprivation, and accept it—and eventually put it behind
us.

(3) KNOW HOW TO REACH OUT. Maybe your
parent was too sick, too troubled to use the help
that was available; but you can get help when you
need it: useful, unintimidating, *strengthening* help
—SO YOU DON'T HAVE TO GET STUCK
THE WAY YOUR PARENT DID.

(4) LOOK FOR SOMETHING POSITIVE in the
parent who's evoked so much hate and pity. Believe it or not, there is something, probably more

than one thing, that's good about that parent that you can identify with. The point is, you won't have to focus so much on the pathology (the suicide, the rape conviction, the irresponsibility, the ugliness) if you can see some of the good of that parent in you. Maybe it's a musical talent that you share, or beautiful eyes, or a rich sense of humor. Maybe it's a memory of earlier, less troubled times when he/she showed real tenderness. You don't have to be goody-two-shoes to find a good "mental souvenir" of that parent; you only have to be willing to look.

Chapter 30: "I'M ALWAYS AFRAID."

(When the anger gets out of hand.)

It's pretty clear-cut: you read in the paper that a little kid was beaten or stomped or stuffed in the oven, and you *know* that's child abuse.

But did you also know that excessive anger in a parent doesn't have to reach the physical stage in order to qualify as child abuse. "Even yelling can be considered child abuse," says a mother who has sought help for her own overly aggressive treatment of her daughters.

Physical abuse *is* one form, and surely one that's receiving increasing attention on the TV news. It is being reported much more now, which is great because it helps the young victim and it also helps the abusing parent (who is sick and needs help, or he/she wouldn't be doing it). This is encouraging because the idea of being pushed around, smacked, kicked, or beaten by a parent, of all people, is ugly and frightening for everyone concerned.

There are other forms of abuse, too. Some of them are subtle in that the bruises may not show. But they are deeply felt nonetheless.

- There is *physical neglect,* for example, in which the parent or parents fail to provide proper clothing, food, medical attention, and routine body care.
- There is the deadly, passive indifference from parent to child that we call *emotional deprivation.*

179

- There is *verbal assault,* which takes place when a parent uses words to hurt and humiliate instead of fists or other weapons.
- There is *sexual abuse,* which encompasses any sexual contact between adult and child.
- And finally there is *emotional abuse,* which is the inevitable side effect of every other form of abuse, and characterized by a feeling, on the victim's part, of *growing up worthless in an atmosphere of hate.*

So much of the bad stuff seems to come from anger and frustration on the parent's part.

- Why are some parents always yelling at their young people?
- Why are certain ones always on a fine edge, ready to explode over nothing?

It doesn't mean they're monsters or sadists. In fact, parents who attack kids verbally or physically aren't doing it deliberately—on purpose, by design—but because they have just reached a personal **boiling point** and are out of control.

Take Brendan's father, for example: "I guess my dad's nice a lot of the time," Brendan muses. "But when he's tired or pressed, and especially if he's been drinking, I can practically see him building up to a rage.

"When it does come out, it's always over something trivial and stupid. Like last week when my hands were wet, and I didn't get a good grip on the milk carton. So I dropped it and it spilled all over the kitchen floor. He called me disgusting, clumsy, worthless, and a four-letter word. The way he screamed at me, you'd think I'd burned the house down or killed my sister. I mean, he made me feel like a *criminal.*"

It may well be that Brendan's father (along with hundreds of thousands of other fathers in all walks of life, all across the socioeconomic board) is only doing what

was done to *him* when he was a boy. He might have been made to feel that clumsiness (or other minor human flaws) were unpardonable sins, blemishes, *insults to the parent!* Brendan's father never learned that there could be other, better, kinder ways of dealing with stress and annoyance, other ways of expressing displeasure without demolishing the son he loves.

Neither Brendan, nor you, can change a parent's history or make him/her into something else. But any young person living with a parent as explosive as Brendan's father *does* have the option of cutting down some on the extent, the frequency, and the ferocity of the rampages.

Removing red flags. One simple selfhood preservation technique is to reduce the predictable provocations. For example, if you keep your sneakers off the stairs where your quick-to-anger parent would otherwise trip on them (again); if you keep your room (or your clothing, or your life) relatively orderly; then you may not be such a convenient, handy *target* for the waxy yellow build-up of *anger*—at least some of the time.

Steering clear. By now you should know some of the early storm signals, right? After a week of working overtime? After being laid off? After drinking? After a fight with the other parent? Maybe you don't know the *reason,* but you can see it coming on. Know when to get *yourself* out of the way: when to go to your room (or out of the house) instead of standing there, fascinated/frozen like a deer in the glare of onrushing headlights.

Know when it's useful to cater. Let's say you and your sister like to listen to records before dinner; it's your relaxation to play them loud. But then your mother comes home from work, sore as a boil, complaining, maybe cursing the loudness, threatening to bust the records—or the stereo—or you.

Well, you could sass her, turn it louder, and let her know that you have rights, too. But it might make more *sense* to recognize that she is not attacking you personally so much as reacting to accumulated stress, frustrations, and so on; that she craves quiet at the end of the day. It's not up to you to make up for her problems, but at least an appearance of some sympathetic understanding (in the form of a little peace and quiet by her standards at coming-home time) might go a long way towards defusing an ongoing source of motherly fury-at-you.

Communicate. Assuming that your parent is calm and approachable at least some of the time, pick a good opportunity to say, "Look, you can criticize me when I'm wrong, but I really feel awful when you call me names (or scream in my face . . . or tell me I'm a worthless slut).

WELL, YOU DON'T HAVE TO
CALL ME NAMES

I know you don't necessarily mean all you say to me, but it still hurts my feelings."

This is more likely to get the results you want than a hackle-raising accusation or generalization would, as in, "You've always treated me like dirt. You're a rotten parent."

Watch yourself. Check to make sure you aren't sometimes provoking the extraordinary unpleasantness at home. It's true: many young people do. No, they're not crazy. It's because, in many families, the abusive tirade is followed by a sort of double-take of such *remorse* and *loving concern* and *tenderness* that the young person gets almost addicted to phase two and unconsciously *invites* phase one (with all its accompanying ego-damage and pain) in order to be sure of getting the closeness of phase two. A very poor deal when you think about it!

Watch out again. Check yourself for a tendency to deny or not let yourself see any fault in the parent who acts so mean or blows up so easily. This way, you make *yourself* out to be the "bad guy," as if you deserve any and all of the psychological (or physical) punishment you're getting. This is a significant temptation to many young people who find it *too* threatening to face the real possibility that they are living with a parent who is unfair or unreasonable or unable to control the attacks.

Remember: you can try to help cut down on the angry-confrontation count between you and your parent, but don't expect your influence to change the parent's basic way of looking at the world. (That would be too big an order.)

DON'T JUST SIT THERE; When a parent's anger gets to be more than you can handle, it's not enough to merely hope that it will go away soon. Trust that nervous feeling in your gut and GET SOME HELP. There *is* an adult you can rely on and confide in. Maybe it's a relative, or a favorite teacher, or your best friend's mother or father. Maybe it's someone you work for. A clergyperson or family doctor will step in if you ask him/her to, to offer whatever protection you need. BUT YOU HAVE TO LEVEL. The point is, if you feel like an explosion's on the way, you're probably right. And you aren't helping anyone, least of all yourself, by merely waiting for the worst to happen.

Chapter 31: THE BEST-KEPT SECRET

(Sexual Abuse By A Parent)

You hear the term "molesting" and you picture some ignorant, filthy drunken lout forcing his way into his daughter's bedroom; doing his worst; then threatening death if she breathes a word. Sometimes, of course, that *is* the way it is; but often it isn't.

- Plenty of well-mannered, educated, sober parents sexually abuse their children.
- *Boys* are victims, too.
- It doesn't have to be "all the way" to qualify as sexual abuse. Fondling, stroking, and even *talking* in a sexually provocative way are also sexual abuse.
- It doesn't have to be violent, or forced, in order to qualify. It is *still* exploitive, inappropriate, and wrong. IT IS STILL DAMAGING TO THE CHILD (even a teenaged child!).
- It doesn't have to feel *bad*. It may even seem like fun—at first. Maybe it is exciting, sexually gratifying—or maybe you just enjoy the physical closeness, the hugs and the warmth. Perhaps that "special relationship" with the parent gives *you* a sense of special importance. NEVERTHELESS, there can be a "time-bomb effect in cases of incest." According to social worker Maddi-Jane Sobel and sociologist Linda C. Meyer, "It is not unusual for vic-

185

tims to develop problems later in life . . ."

What is sexual abuse?

Basically, it is a distortion of normal behavior. Physical affection between a parent and his son or daughter is not only nice and warm, but an important part of family life. Without any hugging and kissing and cuddling, we'd all be terribly cold fish. But when a parent's (or stepparent's) caresses become:

- too lingering—
- too seductive—
- too exciting—
- too interfering—

when the adult engages in the touching or nuzzling of private parts or consciously stimulates the younger person, IT IS OUT OF BOUNDS AND UNACCEPTABLE. If it makes you uncomfortable (even a pat on the hand or the head with a certain meaningful look can be too much!), then it is A VIOLATION OF YOU.

No matter how low-key or mild or fleeting the event, no matter how willing or eager a participant you have been, YOU DO NOT NEED TO FEEL RESPONSIBLE OR GUILTY. It is completely the adult's fault and not at all your fault, because it is the adults who are supposed to keep that sort of thing from happening. FEELINGS, WISHES, AND DESIRES ARE NEVER BAD. ACTING ON THOSE IMPULSES CAN BE.

Submitting to sex with a parent can make you feel extremely bad about yourself: used, dirty, immoral, crazy. Those feelings are normal, but the fact that what's happened has happened, REFLECTS NOTHING BAD ABOUT YOU, ONLY SOMETHING DESPERATELY SAD AND OUT OF CONTROL IN THE PARENT. *AND IT IS IMPERATIVE THAT YOU SEEK HELP IN GETTING THE PROBLEM STOPPED.*

You can do some research: find out who (which agency, which police unit, which social worker, for example) investigates charges of abuse in your community. Some are enormously sympathetic and helpful, some less so.

There's one place, for example, the Joseph J. Peters Institute (formerly the Center for Rape Concern in Philadelphia), that has one of the best approaches because they understand the complicated feelings and problems that can *cause* a parent to molest a son or daughter— and the effects it can have on **each member of the family.** At the center, they work to help ". . . the victim accept and deal with her/his ambivalence, anger, and guilt feelings"; and, in addition, they help to ease the deep and complicated tensions and anxieties affecting the *others* in the family, and to minimize the chance of a repeat. That means straightening out some of the wrongheaded ways that the parents are feeling about themselves, each other, and the children; and even helping nonmolested brothers and sisters to cope with *their* "feelings about the 'family secret' and their hostility towards the victim and/or the offender."

What a lot of young people don't realize is that the emotional trauma of parents messing around with you can stay around even *years after the molesting has stopped.*

Fortunately, there is a self-help group, with many, many chapters across the country. It is called Daughters and Sons United, and it is for young people who have been sexually abused by a parent or other close relative.

If you would like to know about a DSU group in your area, where you could gather some moral support and comfort from others who've had similar experiences, send a self-addressed stamped envelope to:

Daughters and Sons United
840 Guadalupe Parkway
San Jose, CA 95110.

On breaking the cycle.

The people who've studied child abuse, in all forms, state that it's almost always a cyclical problem, which means a problem that tends to go on from generation to generation . . . to generation.

Unless, of course, it's stopped.

Even under the best of circumstances—when you're loaded with great resources, and when you've had a splendid upbringing—parenting *still* is a very complicated, hard, and draining job.

IT'S CRUCIAL NOT TO FALL INTO THE TRAP OF HAVING A BABY VERY EARLY IN LIFE in the false hope that the baby will somehow "make up" for the love you never got enough of from your parents. It doesn't work out. It makes everything harder. Love *doesn't* conquer all. Learning—and understanding—can help. Nobody is born with good parenting skills. If you have been abused, the chances are good that you will need to *learn* better methods than the ones that were practiced on you before you can consider yourself to be "good parent material."

By the way, if you're already a parent and not entirely happy with your ways of dealing with the pressures, you might want to think about the national self-help group known as Parents Anonymous. It is *not,* as some people think, just for people who have harmed their children. The group works well, members say, as *an ounce of prevention,* before any harm is done. It can be a good way to *unlearn some of the bad patterns* you had to grow up with, and replace them with more benign, more constructive responses.

To find a local chapter, check your phone book under Parents Anonymous: or you can reach a local chapter by calling 1-800-421-0353 (outside of California) or 1-800-352-0386 (within California).

Chapter 32: EXTRA HELP

(Sources you might not have considered up to now.)

In the preceding chapters, we've mentioned a number of organizations and groups geared to helping with one kind of family problem or another. Here are some other suggestions. While you'll see that they range quite a bit in style and format, what they have in common is that none of them are mere "crutches." All are meant to call upon and strengthen *you and your own ability to cope,* because the more good coping techniques you can add to your repertoire, the better your chances are for overcoming the steady drain on you and all the other pressures involved in living with a parent whose problems are overwhelming.

I. Taking charge.

No matter what's happened to you, and no matter whether you opt to seek outside help (from peers or from professionals, or from whomever), the point is that you are now at a crossroads of sorts.

You've seen your parents' imperfections—maybe serious ones; you've felt the pain. But now it's up to you to decide whether, as a result of the problems and the things in your childhood that didn't go exactly right, you're going to let yourself drift along—maybe getting into trouble, maybe just never quite getting (or being) what you wanted; and just shrugging and blaming it on

depriving parents or overindulgent parents or absent
parents or hovering ones who never let you off the leash.
**That's one choice. The other is to take the bull by the
horns** at this point and see what you can do to reach the
goals that are important to you, whatever they are.

It takes commitment . . . and practice . . . and a whole
lot of persistence to turn self-pity and resentment into a
more constructive— and more *rewarding*—approach.
Maybe you can get some good encouragement and practical help from "Toughlove for Teens." That is an off-
shoot of Toughlove, the fairly new program for parents
troubled by their teenagers' behavior. Toughlove for
Teens is an even more recent and experimental support
group designed to teach teens how to take responsibility
for themselves with the help of other teenagers. Right
now, it's only operating locally, in Pennyslvania. But
you can write to find out what a sample meeting would
be like or for pointers on getting your own Toughlove
for Teens group organized.

> Send a self-addressed, stamped envelope to:
> Lee Rush
> c/o Community Service Foundation
> P.O. Box 70
> Sellersville, PA 18960.

*II. "I know exactly how you feel" . . . a one-on-one ap-
proach.*

Self-help *groups* can be great for many people, much
of the time. Sometimes, it can by itself be enough, or
even better, or good *in addition,* to talk just with one
individual, a kind of "buddy," someone who's "been
there" in the sense of having or having recently had first-
hand experience with a problem or cluster of problems
to match your own.

Using this concept, the Lutheran Social Services of North Dakota started a program known as "Friends." Not to be confused with Quakers, this group of Friends is a network of individuals who have lived through all kinds of major crises, both personal and family. Each one has not only experienced it, but also, according to Reverend Keith D. Ingle, the program's coordinator, "managed to achieve some degree of positive resolution" about it.

The way it works, is that each participant is matched up (or "beFRIENDed") with another person in similar straits. What they have to offer each other is not just what Reverend Ingle calls "a listening ear and a voice of experience," but also understanding, acceptance, empathy, and a chance to see the situation clearly, to discuss what might or might not be a good course of action. A **friend,** Reverend Ingle stresses, doesn't attempt to solve problems for you—or even tell you how. Rather, it's all in the spirit of "I'll-help-you-to-help-your-self."

They are careful not to overtalk (as in "I'll tell you all about it; just listen to my insights") or to overadvise (as in "I'll tell you exactly how you've got to handle that") or to dig (as in "I want you to open up all your closets and uncover all your dark secrets").

While the Friends program itself is, unfortunately, limited to residents of North Dakota, there's nothing to stop you from borrowing their idea and seeking a "Friend" of your own through your own contacts, the local grapevine, or an acquaintance of an acquaintance, whose problem seems to mirror your own. (P.S. Maybe this would be a great time to make a friend—and a FRIEND—out of the brother or sister you always used to fight with or ignore.)

"I WANT OUT"

Sometimes parents behave so badly that the desire to be out from under changes to an overwhelming urge. *Should* you take off?

Of course, you're longing to make your own decisions; to live without anybody checking up on you or nagging.

And maybe you're having an impossible time convincing your parents that you're not a little kid.

Running away might seem like a way of achieving Instant Adulthood (not to mention plenty of Real World Adventure for a change). BUT. . . .

- It's better for your own growth (*and* future family harmony) for you to stay and *work out* the conflicts and the problems—whatever they are.

- The world out there might *look* like an oyster, but look again: What happens when you run out of money? Get hungry? Get cold? Get sick? Get lonesome? There are all kinds of unfriendly people out there: pimps, pushers, perverts, to name a few, who make a career out of preying on young people who don't have a parent/rescuer waiting in the wings.

If you want an expert opinion, why not contact the National Runaway Switchboard? Its toll-free number (800-621-4000) is open 24 hours a day; and you can call them for an absolutely honest and confidential picture of what it's really like to be on the loose.

If you're craving more Real World Responsibility in your life, you might consider volunteering at a local crisis center, hospital, or other place where people who are suffering can go for help.

If school seems to stretch out before you as Protracted-Childhood-Without-End,   you might want to think about getting done with high school and then taking off a year before college.

If you want to make it really exciting and memorable, you might use that year to join VISTA (that's Volunteers In Service To America, otherwise known as the domestic Peace Corps). The fact that you need to be over eighteen to be eligible for VISTA, by the way, suggests something about the level of maturity you need before you can realistically hope to go out there and make it.

III. The pros: trained and experienced sounding boards.

For teenagers only. There is a nice, low-key kind of professional help available:

- if you can't bear the thought of a so-called "shrink."
- if you wish there was someone you could see once, or now and then, for a *quick* consultation (and, consequently, a *small* fee).

What we're talking about is the adolescent specialist —not a psychologist or psychiatrist, but a physician who's been specially trained to concentrate on the whole mixed bag of emotional, as well as physical concerns of adolescents.

There are hundreds of adolescent specialists now who

make a point of being warmly and wisely available to their patients (privately, without a parent in the room with you) at any stage of a problem—especially before it's hatched into anything concrete.

If you would like a list of the adolescent specialists in your state, send a self-addressed, stamped envelope with a note to:
　　The Society for Adolescent Medicine (SAM)
　　P.O. Box 3462
　　Granada Hills, CA 91344.

For you or the whole family.

Whether *your* parent-problem is one that can be solved or changed, or whether your best bet is to work around it and find ways to make your own situation more bearable, you can get some very good guidance from a "marriage and family therapist." This professional umbrella, so to speak, covers a whole variety of psychologists, psychiatrists, pastoral counselors, and others with a degree in counseling *or* a minimum of an M.A. in a field like sociology, plus at least two years of clinical experience.

Marriage and family therapists will see you by yourself, or, if you prefer, *with* a member or members of your family—or both ways.

If you'd like a list of the ones nearby, write (with self-addressed stamped envelope) to:
　　American Association for Marriage and
　　Family Therapy
　　924 West 9th Street
　　Upland, CA 91786
Or, call their toll-free number, 800-854-9876,

for a local referral anywhere in the United
States.

By the book.

If it's imperative to find help fast, look up Crisis In-
tervention or Hotline in the phone book.

If you'd like to consider using a counselor or therapist
to bolster your strength-in-coping *beyond* an immediate
crisis, you can find some likely prospects by checking in
your phone book under: Mental Health or County Medical Societies, the Department of Child Psychiatry or
Adolescent Psychiatry, or the Adult Psychiatry/ Outpa-
tient Division of any nearby hospital.

BEFORE YOU GET INVOLVED with any self-help
group, helping agency, or clinic, YOU need to feel comfortable. And YOU have a right to know:

- what they do—and what they don't do. For example, do they offer a listening ear and an opportunity
  for you to talk about your problem at home? Or are
  they willing and able to intervene in more concrete
  ways, like providing homemaker services if needed,
  or providing you with some tangible protection
  from a parent who is dangerously ill and violent?
- what kind of training or credentials their staff-
  members have. Are they professionals (such as psychiatrists, psychologists, social workers)? If they're
  volunteers, have they been screened in any way and
  trained to help you, or are they merely there to
  serve some do-gooder need of their own? If it's a
  self-help group, what are the membership require-
  ments?
- how much (if anything) is it going to cost you? Is
  there a set fee? A sliding scale based on parents'

income? Or is it on a pay-what-you-want donation basis?

● whether it's confidential. Can you come to them with the assurance that your privacy will be protected?

THEN. . . .

DON'T make excuses for putting off making that phone call. Today is better than tomorrow; the sooner you reach out for help, the sooner you'll reap the benefits.

DO follow through. You may not hit the right place on the first try. You might even go to a meeting or session that doesn't feel right. Instead of forgetting about the whole thing, try something else. The help is *there*—even if you have to go to a little bit of trouble to find it.

DO bear in mind that one kind of help doesn't automatically rule out another. For example, seeing a family counselor doesn't mean you can't *also* join Alateen, if that applies. Whatever bolsters you and helps you get a handle on coping better is worth the time and energy involved in keeping appointments, facing the problems, and working them out.

Chapter 33: LOOKING BACK/LOOKING FORWARD

Look: *you've really come a long way!* You can successfully steer your way through and around—**and out of** —the power-struggles that sap everybody's strength, like whether or not they have the right to pick your friends or make you pick up your room. You've learned how far a little diplomacy can take you.

Also, you've been able to see your parents—*and their quirky behavior*—in a whole new light. Now you can see where they aren't deliberately trying to embarrass or frustrate you; and, consequently, you can afford to be that much more understanding—sympathetic even— when they act tyrannical or wishy-washy, unbelievably silly or accusing, or whatever.

You've also found some good and useful ways of working on the really major, out-of-control problems— like drinking, for example, and the bad stuff that can go with it; problems that can cast as dark a shadow on your life as anything you'll ever experience. But now you know that you don't have to struggle all alone. There is help. All you have to do is take advantage of it. (And you may be surprised at how much more manageable those gigantic problems can become.)

Some final thoughts to reflect on.

If things have been stormy and tearful up to now, you

can begin to relax, to look forward to relief in the not-too-distant future. According to experts, the truly classic child/parent struggle pattern is shaped like a mountain: highest in the teen years when relations between YOU and THEM are particularly rocky and jagged. But even if you don't do anything special (other than waiting it out), that mountain of discord *does* tend to recede when the rivalry, the disciplinary problems, and those cat-and-mouse games no longer apply. Then you and your parents—who may have been ready to strangle each other yesterday—may actually come to look at each other *tomorrow* (or *sometime* soon) not only with **tolerance,** but also with **respect** . . . and **humor** . . . and even great **affection!**

Maybe you'll never be super-close to them, no matter how much you have wished for it and no matter how gamely you've tried. Sometimes, when parents are very much **stuck** in a serious, debilitating rut of one sort or another, you end up just having to cut your losses and let go.

If that turns out to be the case with yours, at least you can be glad that *you have the choices and options they lacked.* Also, you have ways of getting help when you need it, so that you won't have to go on suffering a deficit because of what they weren't able to give you.

If things have been horrendous, you can still look forward to a very happy life. Psychologists' studies have shown that an unhappy childhood does *not* necessarily point to more of the same as an adult. Time can heal if you are willing to let it. The conflicts and obstacles you've had to deal with may even turn out to be useful in helping you choose to become the kind of adult—and eventually the kind of **parent**—you want to be.

Naturally, you would like to avoid the mistakes that they made; chances are you will be able to obviate most

of them. But keep some perspective. **No one is 100 percent problem-free;** and life is a lot more comfortable once you can truly believe that YOUR PARENTS DON'T HAVE TO BE PERFECT IN ORDER TO BE GOOD—AND NEITHER DO YOU.

    So now it's up to you: to live your life and make decisions, **not** any longer for the sake of pleasing your parents, or for the sake of defying them. But just because, in the last analysis, it's **not** going to be their point of view (or the opposite), but **your** own uncommonly

good

common sense

that works

the best!

ABOUT THE AUTHOR

Jane Marks is a contributing editor to *Seventeen* where she recently co-authored a book with Abigail Wood, based on *Seventeen's* "relating" column.

Ms. Marks is also the author of HELP—A GUIDE TO CONSULTING AND THERAPY WITHOUT A HASSLE (Julian Messner Publishers). Ms. Marks writes for a wide variety of magazines. Her articles on subjects that range from horses and dogs to "the myth of the Super Mom" have led to appearances on a number of radio and television shows including "Donahue."

Ms. Marks is married to an economist and is the mother of two boys.